# Growing through the Stress
# of Ministry

# Growing through the Stress of Ministry

Susan Muto
and Adrian van Kaam

**Resurrection Press**
An Imprint of
**CATHOLIC BOOK PUBLISHING CORP.**
Totowa • New Jersey

First Published in March, 2005 by
    Catholic Book Publishing/Resurrection Press
    77 West End Road
    Totowa, NJ 07512

© 2005 by the Epiphany Association

ISBN 1-878718-96-7

Library of Congress Catalog Card Number: 2004117496

Cover design by Beth DeNapoli

Printed in the United States of America

1  2  3  4  5  6  7  8  9

# Contents

## Other Books of Interest by Susan Muto

Caring for the Caregiver

Celebrating the Single Life: A Spirituality for Single Persons in Today's World.

John of the Cross for Today: The Ascent

John of the Cross for Today: The Dark Night

Late Have I Loved Thee: The Recovery of Intimacy

Pathways of Spiritual Living

Praying the Lord's Prayer with Mary

## With Adrian van Kaam

The Commandments: Ten Ways to a Happy Life and a Healthy Soul

Commitment: Key to Christian Maturity (Text and Workbook)

Divine Guidance: Seeking to Find & Follow the Will of God

Harnessing Stress

Healthy and Holy Under Stress

Practicing the Prayer of Presence

Stress and the Search for Happiness

The Woman's Guide to the Catechism of the Catholic Church

## Other Books of Interest by Adrian van Kaam

The Art of Existential Counseling

Formation of the Human Heart, Volume III
(Formative Spirituality Series)

Fundamental Formation, Volume I
(Formative Spirituality Series)

Human Formation, Volume II
(Formative Spirituality Series

Looking for Jesus

The Music of Eternity: Everyday Sounds of Fidelity

On Being Involved: The Rhythm of Involvement and
Detachment in Human Life

Our Lady of Epiphany

Religion and Personality

Religious Presence of the Christian

The Roots of Christian Joy

Scientific Formation, Volume IV
(Formative Spirituality Series)

Spirituality and the Gentle Life

The Tender Farewell of Jesus: Meditations on Chapter 17 of
John's Gospel

Traditional Formation, Volume V
(Formative Spirituality Series)

Transcendence Therapy, Volume VII
(Formative Spirituality Series)

Transcendent Formation, Volume VI
(Formative Spirituality Series)

The Transcendent Self: The Formative Spirituality of Middle,
Early, and Later Years of Life

The Vowed Life

The Woman at the Well

**With Susan Muto**

Dynamics of Spiritual Direction

Formation Guide for Becoming Spiritually Mature

Foundations of Christian Formation, Volume I
(Formation Theology Series)

The Participant Self

The Power of Appreciation: A New Approach to Personal and
Relational Healing

# Acknowledgments

One definition of the word ministry in the dictionary indicates that it concerns in general any activity that has to do with attending to the wants of others as in volunteering to care for people left homeless after a flood or so alone they lack the courage to carry on. It also means specifically to furnish aid or to provide for others' needs as a humane and Christian servant would.

Admittedly we most often think of a minister as a person who performs a religious function, but for our purposes in this book we want to widen its meaning from a mode of performance to an encompassing presence that overflows into acts like offering comfort and being an instrument of deeply meant and felt healing. When this meritorious presence degenerates into a superficial show of concern, stress accelerates on all sides.

The question is: Can we grow through the inner and outer turmoil associated with the services we offer or does the stress of ministry, ranging from physical exhaustion to spiritual aridity, take more out of us than we have to give? Lacking enough balance in our lives may cause us to "rust out," if not "burn out" altogether. We often hear people who have been in this field for any length of time saying they cannot wait to retire. The pressures upon them are so depleting it seems almost impossible for them to continue in their ministry beyond a certain age.

Experience tells us that if we do not grow through the stresses our ministerial roles place upon us, we may atrophy interiorly while pretending to commiserate with others. Our capacity to care shrinks like wool in a washer. We would rather be anywhere in the world than in this kitchen or that office or on the way to yet another meeting, no matter how much others try to convince us that it is crucially important. False attempts to care for others or to cooperate with them with a phony smile plastered on our face only worsen our predicament. Trying to succeed on the arid soil of self-inflation is no solution either. We need to find a way to cope with stress before it diminishes our creativity and erodes our already waning fervor to the point of total depletion. It is our contention that normal stress combined with the rules of good health can facilitate our functioning at a reasonable pace of heartfelt performance without losing our inner peace.

As we embark upon the co-authorship of this book, we want to acknowledge the ministerial efforts of our staff, notably those of Mary Lou Perez, our production assistant, and Vicki Bittner, our business manager, who care so diligently for all of our service-oriented endeavors at the Epiphany Academy. We hope that all who ponder what we write here will be inspired to live up to the accolade bestowed by the Apostle Paul on us as "ministers of a new covenant" (2 Corinthians 3:6). May the Spirit equip us and the companions of Christ we cherish to dedicate ourselves anew to the gracious and glorious ministry entrusted to us.

Last but not least, we offer a word of thanks to the Board of Directors of our Epiphany Association. Their generous support of the mission and ministry of our Academy of Formative Spirituality, headquartered in Pittsburgh, Pennsylvania, has made this publication possible.

# Introduction

"Enough already! I have more meetings scheduled than the time to attend them! Why should I slave over yet another program for the same people who come to everything? What's to become of me when labor outpaces leisure?"

Laments like these make caregivers feel more like "human doings" than "human beings." The dissonance, depreciation, and depletion associated with loss, bereavement, and job turnover, with separation, divorce, and broken relationships put ministry itself under the microscope of stress-related illnesses. These and similar examples prove that we are all in some way faced with a serious predicament that affects us mentally, emotionally, and spiritually. A frequent lament we hear is that "no matter how much we do the results are so meager." The covenant component of our ministry seems to evaporate in thin air. A few good results do not offset our feelings of failure.

This book does not pretend to treat the diseases associated with hypertension and the downswing from normal to abnormal stress. We have covered these topics more thoroughly in our trilogy of books titled *Stress and the Search for Happiness; Harnessing Stress: A Spiritual Quest;* and *Healthy and Holy Under Stress.* Our purpose here is to show that we can and must grow not in blessed relief from but in the midst of the stress of ministry. Without its pushes and pulls, we might forget the meaning of our call to follow Christ and carry his cross. The temptation we face daily is to escape the full implications of our consent to be disciples of a Master who found no place to lay his head (Matthew 8:20). The Son of God himself showed up at the Samaritan woman's well so tired he could hardly take another step (John 4:6).

However, hopeless it may seem to us when stress is on the rise, we want to show that we can and ought to grow through this gift of God to us. The power of divine grace forms, reforms, and transforms our ministry when obstacles become openings to praise and appreciation; when burdensome tasks prove to be blessings in disguise; when in the humiliation of seeming failure we celebrate the power and glory of God; when the cross of stress, joyfully carried, becomes for us and all those entrusted to our care a sign of renewed fidelity and abandonment to the mystery.

We pray that what we share in the chapters to follow will give everyone who ministers to individuals or groups in need of care these and many more reasons to sing with the psalmist:

> May the glory of the LORD abide forever,
>     and may the LORD rejoice in his works
> When he looks at the earth, it quakes;
>     when he touches the mountains, they smoke.
>
> I will sing to the LORD as long as I live;
> I will sing praise to my God while I have life.
>     May my meditation be pleasing to him,
> for I find my joy in the LORD.
>     May sinners be banished from the earth,
> and may the wicked no longer exist.
>
> Bless the LORD, O my soul.
>
> Alleluia.
>
>                                    (Psalm 104:31-35)

# A Minister's Prayer

*Lamb of God,*
*When I grow weary with strain of work, high stress,*
*Guide me to sweet meadows of presence,*
*Lovely oases in wastelands of inhumane worlds.*

*Gentle Master,*
*When I feel wounded, lonely, forlorn,*
*Call me home to fields of grass green, pristine,*
*Symbols of hope amidst despair, lack of care.*

*Staff of Life,*
*When I push against the pace of grace,*
*Comfort me with warm embrace, calming as cool breezes,*
*Waves of welcome peace soft as night air.*

*Good Shepherd,*
*When I cannot find words to preach, guide, teach,*
*Draw forth from my heart truths to console abandoned souls*
*With blessings flowing like water down slopes of melted snow,*
*Giving comfort to the lowly,*
*Courage to the faint of heart,*
*Peace to the afflicted,*
*Light to people groping*
*in dark thickets*
*of doubt and despair,*
*Good news for young and old,*
*lean and spare,*
*all those entrusted to my care.*

*May I be your minister in friendly homes and foreign lands,*
*Laying hands on those sick in body and in soul,*
*Making whole the broken, humble-hearted,*
*Leaving behind the ninety-nine*
*To seek the lost and tempest-tossed,*
*Those being born and those at heaven's door,*
*All this I pray, in your name, O Lord!*

—Susan Muto and Adrian van Kaam

# 1

# Laying to Rest Ministerial Distress

*On one occasion our good Lord said:* Every kind of thing will be well; *and on another occasion he said:* You will see yourself that every kind of thing will be well. *And from these two the soul gained different kinds of understanding.*

*One was this: that he wants us to know that he takes heed not only of things which are noble and great, but also of those which are little and small. . . . And this is what he means when he says: Every kind of thing will be well.*

*For he wants us to know that the smallest thing will not be forgotten. Another understanding is this: that there are many deeds which in our eyes are so evilly done and lead to such great harms that it seems to us impossible that any good result could ever come of them. And we contemplate this and sorrow and mourn for it so that we cannot rest in the blessed contemplation of God as we ought to do. And the cause is this: that the reason which we use is now so blind, so abject and so stupid that we cannot recognize God's exalted, wonderful wisdom, or the power and the goodness of the blessed Trinity. And this is his intention when he says: You will see yourself that every kind of thing will be well, as if he said: Accept it now in faith and trust, and in the very end you will see truly, in fullness of joy.*

*And so in the same five words said before: I may make all things well, I understand a powerful comfort from all the works of our Lord God which are still to come.*

—Julian of Norwich

"The harder I try the behinder I get." Remember that old saying? It suggests that our approach to ministerial stress may be off the beam. We want to rid ourselves of it, to lead tranquil lives, not to be bothered by so many problems. Perhaps it is time to take another approach: to lay this stress to rest by befriending it, to stop fighting our full schedules and learn to accept the challenges placed before us daily without complaints or regrets, trusting in the sacred pledge the Lord God made to the medieval mystic of Norwich that *all will be well.*

Modern life, from urban sprawl to the smallest village, makes relentless demands upon us. Technology that was supposed to save us time costs us more time everyday. Once we let go of our naive expectation that life without any stress would be perfect, we may begin to read the text of daily life with formative wisdom. We may see in it signs of God's providential call.

By entering into the dynamics inherent in every caregiving event, we feel a new sense of accomplishment. Banished are the politics of self-centered cleverness. Befriended is the mystery of binding our gifts and talents to a sustaining presence that shepherds us through the most trying circumstances. Christ forgives our faults. He shows us the way to complete what we started in a gracious and effective manner, full of mercy and self-giving love.

Ironically the distress we feel melts like ice on a warm day when we allow it to disclose the direction in which Christ asks us to go. Just as plants grow stronger when the soil around them is raked and fertilized, so we may bloom where we are planted and advance to new heights of spiritual and social maturity through the stress of ministry.

This shake-up disrupts our complacency. It is an unmistakable mark of maturation in Christ. Gentle yet firm nudgings by the Spirit set us on a fresh path to ministerial effectiveness. What we do flows from who we are. The Spirit purifies our hearts of overly stressful feelings of frustration, impotence, and irritation. Service becomes inseparable from contemplative presence to the Sacred.

The task of Christian ministry is a gift and an endowment that only the vivifying Spirit can bestow on our heart. No forced smile can substitute for this grace of inner transformation. From parish pews to the offices of professionals in every walk of life, from households to corporate centers, we realize that our inspiration to serve can only come from on high. We trust that if the wind and the seas listen to the Lord, he will be with us always and that we need not be afraid of the forces of evil that rage in any godless society (cf. Mark 4:35-41).

### Seeking Transformation of Heart

The dynamic strivings and expressions characteristic of ministry in Christ flow from five centralizing dimensions of our life as created, redeemed, and sanctified by the Trinity. In the New Testament the Holy Spirit, often called the *pneuma*, chooses the *ecclesia* (the Church) as his Bride. This highest pneumatic-ecclesial dimension of our Christian personhood suggests that all of us in some way are handmaidens of the Lord. Our ministry leads to deepening surrender to him and a true change of heart.

1. Our *pneumatic dimension* makes us more receptive to the *inspirations* that come to us as gifts of the Holy Spirit, who lovingly outpours into our contemplative core the lights and insights that enable us to care enough to continue to offer generous and charitable service, even when the odds are stacked against us.

2. From our *transcendent dimension* comes the tendency of our heart to be formed by and to give form to *aspirations* for the "More Than." This dimension frees us to go more deeply into our eternal call in God and to go beyond whatever hampers its fulfillment in our admittedly still shallow hearts. Such transcendence enables us to turn idealistic pledges to pursue true ministerial excellence in Christ's name into realistic projects.

3. The dynamic strivings of our *functional dimension* prompt the arousal of wise and prudent Spirit-guided *ambitions,*

without which we might lack the stamina to perform the many tasks asked of us both personally and professionally. We do so for the greater glory of God, never for lesser motives like the promotion of our own sense of power.

4. The *pulsions* of our *vital dimension* refer to the im*pulses* or com*pulsions* that have to be carefully appraised to determine what really motivates our ministry. These powerful drives need to be in tune with our longing for God on the higher levels of our being. Pulsions then energize our choice of moderate ministerial goals and temper our tendency to push for dramatic changes.

5. *Pulsations* are part of our *sociohistorical dimension*. They account for our attraction to or repulsion from the trends, fads, and fashions passing through our environment under the impact of the media. Our responsibility is to discern which of these pushes and pulls may cause normal stress to escalate into abnormal distress and its overflow in contrived shows of superficial care.

In general, the lower dimensions of our life (notably, the sociohistorical, vital, and functional) only receive their ultimate meaning and purpose when they are guided by and integrated into *transcendent aspirations* and *pneumatic-ecclesial inspirations*. The pulsation to acquire possessions, the pulsion to feel pleasure, and the ambition to gain power must all be servants of our highest calling to live in increasing conformity to the Christ-form of our soul.

If there is any lesson Christian ministry teaches us it is that we are not made to do it ourselves! Our call is as unique as it is communal. Together with others we are in conversation with an ever-changing human and cosmic world. No one can deny how stressful these unending transitions can be. Be that as it may, we have been invited by grace to transform this world into the house of God, the body of Christ. We must learn to live our ministry not in isolation from but in interaction with others in the providential places where we find ourselves as servants of the Lord.

To grow in spiritual maturity, we need to listen to life–all of life–in the light of our pneumatic-ecclesial dimension. We need to hear God's voice addressing us in the ordinary concert of existence with its stresses and distresses, its consonant and dissonant chords. All that we see and hear attunes us to the field of presence and action that is the arena in which our ministerial life follows its divinely destined course of action.

## Reforming Our Spheres of Existence

We can think of our lives as an intertwining constellation of various spheres of existence. They influence our unfolding in formative and deformative ways, all of which are subject to reformation by Father, Son, and Holy Spirit.

As we reflect on the mystery of God's love, it is natural to look within. Our intraformative sphere represents our rich and complex inner life. It is the place of the heart where we may remember, imagine, and anticipate all that we are now and all that God invites us to be in the future.

Creation is also interformational. Our interformative sphere represents the influences we have on one another in family and community life, in our places of labor and leisure. We need a vigilant heart to cope with the stresses that accompany our being with others in a world often empty of meaning. We are always immersed in private and public encounters that both form and deform our lives. Some move us towards our unique-communal call or away from it. Certain interactions may be harmful, others helpful for our growth in ministerial excellence for Christ's sake.

Our *outer immediate* or *situational sphere* of formation accounts for the people, events, and things in our everyday environment that directly affect our capacity to act in accordance with the direction we receive from the Holy Spirit through the *ecclesia* and our here-and-now place in God's plan. We cannot escape the potentially formative or deformative influences of the immediate situations in which we find ourselves; they are an integral part of our formation; they affect the ways we are disposed to live and act as disciples of Christ commissioned by him to bring his word to every nation and circumstance on earth (cf. Mark 16:15).

The *outer mediated* or *wider world* sphere of formation indicates that we are influenced by happenings and forces of which we are not immediately aware. Our life is affected by much that is beyond our personal influence and our direct powers of observation and control. To serve others wisely we need to dialogue with directives disclosed intraformatively as well as interformatively, through our everyday situations as well as through the history of cosmos and humanity. All of these internal and external dynamics interact with one another. Together they form a field of intertwining forces of human and divine formation essential to ministry.

### Deflating Ministerial Distress

Heeding the sacred depth of our life direction demands openness to past, present, and future invitations, challenges, and appeals. Accepting the fact of ministerial stress and making the best of it signifies our option to trust in the Lord, as Julian of Norwich says, "for certainty and strength against every tribulation."

The more our spiritual life matures, the more we are able to behold life as a pattern of providential events. When we view our whole course of development during moments of recollection, we see that our Master Designer has woven a tapestry of revelations about the meaning of our life. Despite the pain and suffering it may have entailed, we have the assurance that "all will be well." Everything we have done conveys a significance beyond what we may have failed to decipher in the stress of the moment.

One lasting disposition of the heart that deflates ministerial distress is humility; it fosters the aspiration to depend on God for whatever good we do and to show compassion for everyone. In many faith and formation traditions, the terms *humility* and *openness* are used almost interchangeably. Humility removes barriers to accepting the limits in ourselves and others; openness is a necessary condition for growth in the other-centered love Christ asks of us. As soon as we try to listen to God's voice within our hearts, our pride-form drives a wedge between us and others. It enflames such deformative dispositions as envy and arrogance; it tempts us to rebel against the commandments and the beatitudes. Sooner or later we are tempted to play "god" and to deny our limits. Holy Scripture often depicts this predicament as stemming from a hardened heart that must be broken open by the amazing grace of God. The psalmist prays for this favor, saying:

> Do not place your trust in extortion,
> and set no vain hopes in stolen goods;
> no matter how greatly your wealth increases,
> do not set your heart on it.
> One thing God has revealed;
> two things have I heard:
> that power belongs to you, O God,
> and so does kindness, O LORD.
> You reward each person
> in accordance with his deeds.
>                                         (Psalm 62:11-13)

The love of Christ in our heart is meant to flow out in the tenderness and mercy that radiate through our matching character. To become ministers of the Word, we need to let ourselves be embraced by God's caring presence and then pass this warmth on to others. The capacity to do so is not the result of our own forced efforts but a response to the grace of God. To grow in consonance with this divine initiative, we need to listen with full attention to the unique-communal call intended for us from all eternity.

As our here-and-now ministry gradually becomes attuned to the Christ-form within us, we may experience a newly found readiness to respond gently and firmly to the stresses the Holy

Spirit sends us in the disguise of occasional suffering. Without any kind of coercion, we may begin to mirror the mystery of Divine Mercy. Our service to others becomes a steady reflection of Christ's sacrificial care for abandoned souls everywhere.

Sustained amidst stress by our oneness with Christ, we may radiate, in ways unplanned and unanticipated, a depth of compassion others recognize as flowing from a Source beyond ourselves. Its epiphanic light softens the hard edges of ministerial stress and enables us to concentrate on becoming "little words" in the Divine Word.

Living in this appreciative manner requires a lot of courage. The French word for the heart, *le coeur*, reminds us that *courage* is a key disposition we ought to cultivate. It takes courage to remain faithful to who we are called to be; to exercise patience in constantly changing situations; to reach out and touch others in their suffering. As courageous ministers of Christ, we strive to use our gifts and skills to the fullest extent and to be with and for others in their need. We want at one and the same time to function at the peak of our performance and to place all that we are and do at the disposal of the Sacred whose servants we are.

## Questions for Reflection

1. Can you think of a time in your life when your direction seemed so obscure that you had only the light at the end of the tunnel to sustain you? What kept you, amidst such stress, from succumbing to distress? Were there any disclosures concerning your calling in Christ that became clearer to you after such a time of upheaval and change?

**Your Thoughts:**

2. Recall a moment when the Holy Spirit granted you a more distinct sense of the pointing of Holy Providence. What caused you to catch a glimpse of the path along which Christ wanted to lead you? How has this clarity helped you to proceed along the stressful roads that loom before you?

**Your Thoughts:**

3. When are you most aware of not being in tune with your unique-communal life call? How do you know that you are on the wrong course? What role does openness to your pneumatic-ecclesial dimension play in this discernment?

**Your Thoughts:**

4.  To be appreciative is to live in praise of the Lord. How does this disposition help to defuse the negative energy found in stressful situations? How does it lighten the burden of stress in your own heart and in the atmosphere in which you live and work?

**Your Thoughts:**

5.  Where do you find the courage to persevere in your ministry despite its distresses? Can you recall a time when you responded to a difficult situation with candor and courage?

**Your Thoughts:**

## Scripture Meditations

**Romans 8:36-39**

As it is written,

> "For your sake we are being killed all
> day long;
> we are accounted as sheep to be
> slaughtered."

No, in all these things we are more than conquerors through him who loved us. For I am convinced that neither death, nor life, nor angels, nor rulers, nor things present, nor things to come, nor powers, nor height, nor depth, nor anything else in all creation, will be able to separate us from the love of God in Christ Jesus our Lord.

**2 Timothy 2:11-12**

The saying is true:

> If we have died with him, we will
> also live with him;
> If we endure, we will also reign with
> him;
> if we deny him, he will also deny us.

### *Meditative Exercises*

What do these texts say to you about overcoming your fear of abandoning yourself to the Mystery in the midst of everyday failures and disappointments?

**Your Thoughts:**

How does the teaching of the Apostle Paul help you to see in every obstacle daily life poses a divinely appointed formation opportunity?

**Your Thoughts:**

# 2

# Shifting from Depletion to Repletion

*Spirit of Love! Descend within me and reproduce in me, as
it were, an incarnation of the Word; that I may be to him
another humanity wherein he renews his mystery.*
                                    —Saint Elizabeth of the Trinity

Ministerial presence is a symphony composed of various
consonant chords or Christ-formed dispositions. Their felici-
tous blend yields a pleasing, compassionate style of presence
and action that is both gentle and firm. Such dispositions may
begin in our mind, but they end as lasting inclinations of our
heart. Its two basic movements are *sensibility* and *responsibility*
which complement one another and account for our *ability* to
minister to others in caring and committed ways. The truly
concerned heart is as reverential as it is effective. Decisions and
actions flowing from it form a benign and balanced blend of
cordiality and rationality.

Such a mixture makes service, even under stress, both
appealing and effective. If we have ever hosted a dinner party,
we know that the lovely ambience we want to create to honor
our guests does not come automatically. For a while we may
feel the pinch of stress, but it subsides the moment our guests
arrive and thank us for such a pleasant expression of hospital-
ity and solicitude for their wellbeing.

As socially sensitive servants of the Lord, we beg for the
grace to remain as tirelessly generous as he was. We want to go
that extra mile to meet the needs demanded by our ministry.

We are ready and willing to do what has to be done within the limits and potentials every situation entails.

Once such social sensitivity becomes an enduring disposition, we are less prone to be depleted by stress. Faced with failure or misunderstanding, we choose with Christ's help not to retaliate in kind but to reveal new channels of creative care. Our appraising mind and our affirming will respond in kind to our compassionate heart. As the integrative center of our Christian personhood, it enables us to grow stronger through the stress of serving Christ in others.

Despite our best intentions, we have to admit that our ministerial presence is at times under too much stress to recover quickly. Although at heart we remain faithful to our commitments, we suspect that our initial fervor is on the wane. We witness a certain ebb and flow in our faith and fervor. We maintain routine dispositions of responsible behavior while sensing that our heart is no longer in what we do. The alternate fading and upsurging of wholehearted engagement can shadow every facet of our ministry from its earliest thrust of dedication to its temporary or permanent deflation.

## Six Phases of the Erosion Process

To understand the seriousness of stress in the context of genuine service, we need to consider the six phases that account for the alternating cycle of fervor and fading interest in the life of any sincere caregiver.

1. *Initial phase of exaltation.* Exalted aspirations and ambitions, strongly influenced by egocentric preoccupations, are prevalent at the start of any ministerial enterprise. They exercise an aggrandizing influence on our imagination. Our service tends to exceed the bounds of common sense. It is overly inflated and elated. The more we experience the practical impossibility of executing our dreams to "save the world, the church, and the people of God," the more these unrealistic expectations prevent us from facing reality. This

stubborn insistence that we can do it alone does not last for long.

2. *Apprehension of dissonance.* We soon begin to sense how stressed we are. What we thought were realistic aspirations and ambitions prove to be unworkable for many reasons. Such initial apprehensions that something is wrong become recurrent, yet they are still widely spaced. We tend to deny the dissonance they evoke, but such blindness is increasingly impossible to sustain.

3. *Significant increase of inner stress.* Peculiar to this phase is that we experience a distinct rise in our stress quotient accompanied by a noticeable erosion of care and concern. As a result of these apprehensions, we can no longer deny the dissonance we feel nor its possible deleterious effects.

4. *Start of a crisis.* The tense push and pull between normal stress and abnormal distress becomes unavoidable. It manifests itself in a waning of inner dedication. In the meantime, we force ourselves to appear to others as perfectly behaved as a trained professional should be, all the while realizing that our motives for caring are fast slipping away.

5. *Resolution of a crisis.* Since we are now fully immersed in a crisis of presence, accompanied perhaps by dour feelings of being utterly abandoned by the mystery, we have to choose between adding to our stress by moving towards a negative solution or tempering it by the beginning of positive response.

The *negative* way only heightens our indifference and inertia. We risk a lasting depletion of social and spiritual presence. Our ability to exercise related modes of routinized religiosity may persist. Especially if our avocation is in the helping professions, we can rely on our training to move us through the motions of ministry, however much our heart is sick with stress. We wonder what is to become of us. "Woe is me" might be the secret refrain of our disgruntled heart.

A *positive* solution to this dilemma entails reaffirmation of our appreciative, hope-filled abandonment to the mystery of forming, reforming, and transforming love. Exalted dispositions tend to come down to earth when we take a more realistic approach to ministry. A side benefit of this positive turn is a lessening of stress, leading us to more effective ways of coping with what triggered this crisis in the first place.

6. *Evolution of a renewed ministerial presence.* As this path opens before us, we close off the prideful assumption that we can find the answers we seek based on our own will power. We turn towards the living wisdom of the faith traditions we espouse. Though we feel less stress, this approach does not free us from the challenges that still lie before us. Similar crises may recur in our lives. Stress and the ideal of sincere Christian service go hand in hand with one another. The more we cling to God, the less anxious we feel. In every crisis, we witness the evolution of an opportunity to follow the "better part" that balances the Mary and Martha in us (cf. Luke 10:38-42).

## Symptoms of Eroded Presence Leading to Depletion

Many physical symptoms may indicate that our ministerial presence has been compromised, including headaches, insomnia, chemical dependency, chest pains, excessive fatigue, backaches, heart and digestive disturbances, skin rashes, repeated colds, and increased susceptibility to a host of other viral infections.

These signs of physical distress are accompanied at times by such emotional upsets as aggravation, irritation, frustration, doubt, and quiet desperation, to say nothing of such sicknesses of soul as dejection and aridity. These spiritual ills further erode the inspiration and efficiency of our ministerial life as a whole.

The most serious consequence of the erosion process is that it may progress to full blown depletion. Its main symptom is inner, not outer, withdrawal, a depletion of presence, not of action. Looking good becomes the mask behind which we hide the fact that our caregiving lacks the will to proceed with courage and candor.

What moves us forward in a forced way are functional benefits. Our career may be in jeopardy! Depleted are the transcendent aspirations and pneumatic inspirations that give meaning to what we do. What cools is our compassion. We become secretly indifferent. We try to hide our angry or resentful feelings behind a wooden grin, but it feels as if our face is about to fall off. Once ministerial presence begins to wane, slovenly actions follow.

Depletion soon leads to a shift in focus from concern for the needs of others to nervous tension about our personal survival. Appearance, popularity, and possible loss of promotion occupy our attention. We insist on looking good, on being pleasing to others, no matter how stressed we feel. We calculate how we can protect and advance our own interests while keeping up the pretense of social concern. As long as we keep busy, we can push away the truth of this transcendence crisis, but sooner or later it catches up with us.

Depletion implies a withdrawal of commitment. It seems temporarily to spare us from the pain of continual disappointment. The loss of ministerial presence and action exacts a high price in physical, emotional, and spiritual exhaustion. Having failed to nip erosion in the bud, it is likely to progress like a fast-moving cancer to full-blown "burn out," but all is not lost. Hope looms on the horizon.

### Reforming Erosion

Faced with the erosion of ministerial presence, we must be willing to ask God to let us find means to halt and reform this process before it gets totally out of hand. Is there a way to "nip it in the bud"? One means of reformation is critical and creative self-examination, aided perhaps by the following questions:

1. Do I live in trusting abandonment to the mystery of formation as ultimately meaningful, however meaningless my
   life now feels?
2. Is my decision in favor of appreciative abandonment
   strong enough to see me through this crisis?
3. Might my very eroded idealism lead me to the threshold of
   a fresh start?
4. How may commitment to Christ in faith, hope, and love
   deepen despite these trials and setbacks?
5. If these virtues have weakened, can I rekindle their flame
   by dwelling in meditative presence on the risen Christ
   whose life I have pledged to celebrate for the good of all?

Prayerful reflection on these and similar questions of our
own devising prevents the erosion process from becoming
worse. Complementing this phase of its reformation may be
practical interventions like vocation counseling and spiritual
direction. Perhaps a change in our type of ministerial engagement may be in the offing. Perhaps the time has come for us to
move to a place or a position more in tune with our own calling in Christ. This mobility factor may mean that our ministry
has to undergo a few alterations if a fresh start is to be found.
Based on what we have learned about our limits and gifts, a
more compelling style of dedication may succeed a former,
more comfortable one. Stressful as these changes may be, walk-
ing down a different road often results in reversal of the erosion
process.

In some instances, effective renewal calls for the assistance
of programs geared specifically to ongoing faith formation. For
example, participation in a direction-in-common group gives
us a chance to put into words the predicament in which we find
ourselves. In the company of like-minded others, we may
become aware of our need to seek support beyond our immediate circle of companions. New friends and acquaintances
facilitate our efforts to reform social presence erosion; they
widen our vision of what we can do to return to dedicated self-
giving with the least amount of stress.

## Repleting Depletion

While we can never do away with the suffering that accompanies Christian ministry nor expect to experience a totally stress-free life, we can prevent depletion from becoming so down-hearted that we lose hope that any of our efforts will succeed. We must believe that we are part of a golden chain of caregivers whose selfless ministry keeps humanity from despair. Our smallest inroads, aided by grace, may rekindle faith in the cross. It reminds us of the indelible link between sanctity and service.

The preventive means we choose to stop erosion from sinking into the quicksand of depletion can be either *effective* or *ineffective*. The latter attempts offer only short-term solutions like a discharge of pent-up feelings. This relief from everyday tensions may offer us an artificial sense of replenishment, accompanied by elated descriptions of the "ideal" social situation that ought to be ours compared to the sad state of the institutions we now serve. The "blame game" escalates with every whiplash of emotional indignation. Instead of preventing depletion, these kinds of sessions only accelerate the process.

One reason for their ineffectiveness is a lack of realistic attunement to the imperfections present in every family circle or faith community. Nothing about sincere ministry puts us in a period of smooth sailing. Stresses like violent storms at sea threaten to cast away the good we have accomplished. Such disappointments may contribute temporarily to the depletion we feel. They tempt us to vent more indignant feelings. These only add fuel to the fire of the depleted spirit that began to burn up our commitment to ministry from the start.

Ineffective repletion sessions may also harm us by playing on our exalted and exalting pride-form. The power of the collectivistic ego may be unleashed if unredeemed by kinder considerations. Mutual expressions of anger and resentment engender imaginary schemes to right every wrong. Pleas for "fixing the system" may be proclaimed in loud speeches, unrelenting position papers, and letters of protest. Rather than alerting us to needed political, social, and ecclesial reform, they dim our chances for inner and outer repletion as a condition for lasting change of heart.

*Effective* repletion sessions aim at change on all levels of our life from initial awakening to inner restoration. We may also foresee the possibility of outer renewal and reform of the institutions we serve. These sessions encourage us to regain our fervor through faith, hope, and love. They help us to be not social-issue but social-presence oriented. A replenished spirit, heart, mind, and will generate more sensitive and responsible ways to diminish stress while enhancing our capacity for Christ-like care and concern.

Such sessions banish the obsessive conviction that we have to wait until certain adverse conditions are removed before we can be spiritually and socially present in justice, peace, and mercy to this wounded world. As long as such absolutized prerequisites dominate our mood, repletion of ministerial presence is unlikely to occur.

Such debilitating "if only" conditions begin to subside when we accept our responsibility to make the best of every situation, even when our best efforts produce meager results. Effective repletion facilitates the insight that by focusing first on our calling in Christ we prevent undue distractions that deplete our energy. We admire and foster the distinctive call of others and witness to the divine guidance we all must follow.

Effective repletion sessions lead to the sober realization that we can never eliminate once and for all the threat of erosion and depletion. The need to keep our stress in check goes hand in hand with any worthwhile ministerial engagement to which we commit ourselves. We learn to be gently alert to whatever forces begin to dry out our dedication. We remain vigilant to the work of the Spirit in us. We cooperate with grace by freely choosing to reform whatever dampens our hope for a deeper, more enduring transformation of life and world in Christ's name.

*Questions for Reflection*

1. Can you give a concrete example of the ebb and flow of social presence in the ministerial situation in which you find yourself? Describe your initial enthusiasm and then ask, "What caused a waning of my concern?"

**Your Thoughts:**

2. Do you remember how you coped with the erosion and possible depletion of social presence in the past? What stresses plague your present experience of ministry? How do "exalted ambitions" play into this process?

**Your Thoughts:**

3. Can you devise a few creative ways to halt the process of eroding social presence and to move from depletion to the repletion of formation energy in any ministerial setting?

**Your Thoughts:**

4.  Assuming that you are trying to be more sensitive to and responsible for the needs of others under your care, how do you minister to them within the limits of your time, energy, and talent?

**Your Thoughts:**

5.  Read the following passages from *Pathways of Spiritual Living* by Susan Muto (Pittsburgh, PA: Epiphany Books, 2004). Then ask yourself, "Why are the spiritual disciplines such important means of stopping the erosion process from degenerating into full-blown depletion? Briefly show how formative reading, meditative reflection, prayer, and contemplation are avenues to ongoing repletion.

> *To be of service is to remain open to surprises, while developing a flow-with–what-comes-and-make-the-best-of-it attitude. Such a realistic approach enables us to cope with the crisis of commitment itself.We can admit what we appreciate and what we resent, what we agree to live with and what we can seek to improve. Rather than letting bad feelings fester, we try to find creative solutions that bring peace to our heart and make peace in a formerly tense situation. Though this crisis may repeat itself, each time it does we can deal with it as a positive challenge, leading to a more lasting sense of dedication. In other words, we seek to disclose Christ's call hidden beneath the superficial upsets found in every professional situation.*
>
> *It is also necessary to open ourselves again and again to the gifts of faith, hope, and love. To believe in the ultimate goodness of life, to hope that things will be better tomorrow than they are today, to love those entrusted to our care–these basic*

*dispositions correct the problems of discouragement, deple-tion of dedication, and closure to compassion. We can be gen-tle and kind because we recognize how vulnerable all of us are. We have to try to live in peace despite the tension that will always be present between the right to be who we are and the real limits of every human situation.*

*If we are at peace within ourselves, not demanding perfec-tion, then we can be peacemakers for others. Christ asks us as his disciples to live peacefully, justly, and mercifully, even if others display opposite tendencies. We can never underes-timate the power of being a living witness to what we believe. In this regard, actions do speak louder than words. People remember who we are, even if they do not recall exactly what we said. What impresses them is our peaceful, just, and compassionate presence.*

**Your Thoughts:**

### Scripture Meditations

## John 15:1-11

I am the true vine, and my Father is the vinegrower. He removes every branch in me that bears no fruit. Every branch that bears fruit he prunes to make it bear more fruit. You have already been cleansed by the word that I have spoken to you. Abide in me as I abide in you. Just as the branch cannot bear fruit by itself unless it abides in the vine, neither can you unless you abide in me. I am the vine, you are the branches. Those who abide in me and I in them bear much fruit, because apart from me you can do nothing. Whoever does not abide in me is thrown away like a branch and withers; such branches are gathered, thrown into the fire, and burned. If you abide in me, and my words abide in you, ask for whatever you wish, and it will be done for you. My Father is glorified by this, that you bear much fruit and become my disciples. As the Father has loved me, so I have loved you; abide in my love. If you keep my commandments, you will abide in my love, just as I have kept my Father's commandments and abide in his love. I have said these things to you so that my joy may be in you, and that your joy may be complete.

## 1 Peter 5:8-10

Discipline yourselves, keep alert. Like a roaring lion your adversary the devil prowls around, looking for someone to devour. Resist him, steadfast in your faith, for you know that your brothers and sisters in all the world are undergoing the same kinds of suffering. And after you have suffered for a little while, the God of all grace, who has called you to his eternal glory in Christ, will himself restore, support, strengthen, and establish you.

## *Meditative Exercises*

1. What do these texts say to you about the need to "prune" those obstacles that hamper your growth in Christ through the everyday stresses your ministry entails?

**Your Thoughts:**

2. What efforts are you making in response to grace to establish the facilitating conditions that best seem to assure your growth in discipleship?

**Your Thoughts:**

# 3

# Seeing the Blessing in Every Burden

*Every day
we should renew our resolve
to live a holy life,
and every day
we should kindle ourselves
to a burning love,
just as if today
were the first day of our new life in Christ.
We should say: "Help me, Lord God,
to fulfill my good intentions
and your holy service.
Starting today,
let me begin perfectly,
for what I have done so far
is nothing.*

—Thomas à Kempis

No disposition as powerfully influences our outlook on life than that of appreciation. Stress stretches us to limits we are loathe to admit. How we cope with physical, emotional, and spiritual burdens is the test of whether we resolve to live a holy life or choose the selfish, ungenerous path to perdition.

The foundational formative triad of infused faith, hope, and love gives us solid ground on which to stand and count our blessings every time we lean towards a depreciative option. To opt in word and deed to live more appreciatively is always a challenge. It is tempting neither to affirm ourselves nor to confirm others as Christ would have us do. Since all is gift, we ought frequently to remember, as the prophet Job did, that "the Lord gave and the Lord has taken away. Blessed be the name of the Lord" (Job 1:21). In this attitude of gratitude, we begin to deal with whatever comes our way in a caring manner, not as the owners but as the stewards of creation. We become joyful people who, even under duress, opt to praise and give thanks for the goodness, truth, and beauty we behold in every person who crosses our path. This splendor, veiled as it is by human sinfulness, breaks like a ray of sun through the clouds of stress that obscure the deepest meaning of our ministry. We remember in faith the cross of Christ. We imagine in love the power of divine forgiveness. We anticipate in hope the world of bliss awaiting us on earth as in heaven. With the psalmist we pray:

> Give thanks to the LORD, for he is good,
>     for his love endures forever.
> Give thanks to the God of gods,
>     for his love endures forever.
> Give thanks to the LORD of lords,
>     for his love endures forever.
>
> He alone works great wonders,
>     for his love endures forever.
> In his wisdom he made the heavens,
>     for his love endures forever.
> He spread out the earth upon the waters,
>     for his love endures forever.
>
> He made the great lights,
>     for his love endures forever.
> He made the sun to rule over the day,
>     for his love endures forever.
> He made the moon and stars to rule the night,
>     for his love endures forever.
>
>                                              (Psalm 136:1-9)

## Practicing the Art and Discipline of Appreciative Appraisal

Our appraisal of life's ups and downs, its peaks and valleys, in praise of the Lord, must begin with awe-filled faith. God must be praised even in the midst of the unexpected turns life takes. Without awe the shift from depreciative to appreciative abandonment is not likely to occur.

Attention is the first fruit of the awe disposition. The awareness of God's presence at the center of our everyday endeavors enables us to see the true significance embedded in our ministerial situation, however stressful our day may be.

These preparatory dispositions of abiding in awe-filled attention enhance our powers of apprehension. In today's language, when we feel apprehensive, it is as if we fear the unknown. We need to be calmed by the Lord's assurance, "Do not be afraid, little flock" (Luke 12:32). Another meaning is equally intriguing. When we apprehend something, we grasp with our mind certain aspects of what, until this moment, had been unknown to us. We need to abide in the inexhaustible wisdom and vastness of God's love. It can only be disclosed to our limited minds in small doses of apprehension, but what a difference they make!

It is because we believe in the breadth and depth of God's care that we can abandon ourselves to the mystery. The gift of appreciative abandonment, based on praise of God's presence in our inmost being, permeates our whole field of formation. We trust God in the face of not knowing or understanding where we are being led.

Once we acknowledge that we are out of tune with the mystery, our honesty itself is an affirmation of the present moment. When we say yes to what it brings amidst the stress we feel, we have reached a decisive transition point in the appraisal process. Here begins our move from a deformative path to a formative one.

As we apply our yes to God in daily life, we find that hope does not desert us however hopeless we may feel. Our faith deepens during a crisis of tension and transition. We start to grow in spiritual maturity. We follow the dance of consonance initiated by Divine Mercy.

Gradual or sudden, predictable or unpredictable, we find ourselves being guided by the ministerial situations where Holy Providence places us. God's will is not "out there" but "there with" the people, events, and things we meet along the way to full Christian dedication. Crises are part of the living tapestry the Master weaves in and with us over a lifetime. We do not know nor can we predict how our final formation story will be woven into the fabric of his plan for each person. We simply trust in the benevolence of our Creator, Redeemer, and Sanctifier while catching brief but telling glimpses of the blessings in every burden.

As we grow through the stress of ministry, we begin to sense that we are part of a salvation story infinitely greater than we are, yet one in which we, too, are privileged to share. We see ourselves in communion with the Divine, with the cosmos and the earth, with our situation and with others. We express our gratitude and thanksgiving for each illuminating event. We witness all that transpires in the light of the Revelation with deep respect for our own and others' unique-communal calling in the Body of Christ.

### Dispositions Enabling Us to Turn Burdens to Blessings

Ministerial stress puts our faith, hope, and love to the test. It tempers illusions of perfectionism. It corrects the myth that life should proceed according to our plans. It reminds us to wait patiently upon the Lord. An attitude of realistic acceptance enables us to cope with crises more smoothly than a posture of control. We learn to acknowledge what we appreciate and what we resent, what we can wholeheartedly confirm and what we must seek to change. Rather than let bad feelings fester, we try to imagine creative solutions to stressful relationships and tense situations. We seek ways to reestablish peace among us, our colleagues and those entrusted to our care. Each time inordinate stress threatens to trample appreciation, we look for creative ways to increase our capacity to turn to Christ, for he is "gentle and humble in heart" and in him we find rest for our souls (Matthew 11:29). The following practices facilitate this lessening of stress:

1. To opt on a regular basis for appreciative abandonment to the beneficial meaningfulness of the mystery. We pray that peace will come to us through the cross of Christ (cf. Colossians 1:20). Beyond the sharp edge of any stressful situation, we seek the truth of what our Lord wants to teach us. Often the cause of our tension is traceable to a weakening of our belief in the sustaining power of God, who holds us in being and strengthens us at every moment for all that we must do and endure.

2. To live the theological virtues of faith, hope, and love and the cardinal virtues of prudence, justice, fortitude, and temperance as the distinguishing marks of our formation in Christ. These gifts and fruits of the Holy Spirit offer us the greatest defense against evil and its cohorts of doubt, despair, and depreciation.

3. To take "fidelity pauses" as soon as we feel pressured. During these blessed breaks, we may discover what it is that God wants us to do. Such respites from ferocious routines create more peace in our heart. They remind us to show mercy in the face of our own and others' vulnerability.

4. To learn to live with the tension that will always be present between the ideal and the real, between our plans and projects and what finally transpires in the reality-testing necessary in any ministerial situation. Our sense of what should be done will always be limited. We must be open to other points of view. If we trust in Divine Providence and strive to cooperate with others without compromising what we believe to be true, our lives in general will be more relaxed and productive.

In addition to these stress-reducing practices, the following core dispositions enhance our commitment to minister to others. Whether our place of work is stormy or calm, our heart has to be in the right place if we want to be an epiphany of Christ's peace.

1.  **Empathic Appreciation.** Empathy means to "feel into" what others are feeling in a heart-to-heart moment. Our countenance itself signals that we empathize with their stressful situation and want to help them through this crisis. Empathy also inclines us to be more compassionate towards ourselves when we get into a like predicament. We experience, at least imaginatively, what others are going through. We accept them where they are. We reverence their dignity and bless their ultimate worth in the light of God's everlasting love for every creature who comes into existence (cf. Jeremiah 31:3).

2.  **Respectful Listening.** Despite widely used techniques of communication, people still complain about neither being heard nor understood. Important as verbal communication is, so too is the art of non-verbal presence. By means of a gesture, a smile, a friendly hug, we can lessen the stress others feel because "no one really listens."

3.  **True Joy.** Most conducive to restoring and maintaining ministerial presence under stress is the disposition of joy. This transcendent gift has to be distinguished from satisfaction on the functional level and pleasure or gratification on the vital level. Joy, as manifested in effective and gracious caregiving, can be felt whether or not we experience little, if any, functional satisfaction or vital gratification. A joyous disposition exuded under stress may only be explicable in the light of the power of appreciation. Such joy is spontaneous; it cannot be forced; it wells up from within our soul. It is present even when we cry on one another's shoulder and wonder what the Lord will ask of us next.

The more these three dispositions become continuous, lasting hallmarks of our ministerial heart, the more what we do will be an expression of the care we have received from our Divine Caregiver. The demands made upon us may not lessen, but we know when to pause to renew our power of appreciation. Issues that place us under stress recede into the background. Questions pertaining to our own survival as humane caregivers come to the fore. Mostly we pray to remain empathic, respectful, and joyful ministers of the Lord, who admit in humility that the repletion of these dispositions is not a luxury but a necessity.

## Restoration of Appreciation

Shared repletion sessions bolster our courage to recommit ourselves to a particular ministry and to ponder our reasons for renewal. The more stressed we feel, the harder it is to sustain our predilection for perfectionism. When projects fail, when trust wanes, when others disappoint us, it is time to let go of our unrealistic expectations. The illusion of being available at all times to all people, while pretending to bear sole responsibility for solving their problems, is the main source of our stress. The tyranny of obsessive ideals fuels the fantasy that we must wipe out single-handedly the adverse conditions causing tension in family life, society, and the faith groupings to which we adhere.

Restored appreciation for our self-worth in God's eyes prevents repletion sessions from degenerating into gloomy arenas of negativity where we harp on how hopeless our ministry is. As we strive with God's help to turn burdens into blessings, we start to notice everyday gifts of warm, deeply felt care. We soon begin to feel more light-hearted. We no longer live in denial of our limits. We laugh at our foolish attempts to be stress-free ministers of the Lord in a flawless situation. Instead we reaffirm our conviction that the erosion and depletion of ministerial presence is a trustworthy pointer to the possibility of repletion and restoration. We catch ourselves as soon as stress turns to distress and quickly put into practice the appreciative abandonment option. We engage in lightning speed appraisal and genuine Christian praise. We heed and better handle the early warning signals of indifference, inertia, and withdrawal by turning useless complaints into invitations to exercise joyous concern.

By advancing a few steps forward we lessen the chances of our falling several more behind. We witness the grace of "just noticeable improvements"rather than mouthing make-believe platitudes but remaining inwardly unchanged. We function more effectively in stressful predicaments. When the strain of ministry weighs upon us, we renew ourselves in the sustaining strength we receive from our encounters with Christ. Without help from on high, we realize that we can do nothing of lasting value. In the end we are only servants of the Divine Caregiver in whose name we offer sustenance and solace to suffering others.

## Appreciative Living in the Lord

To find peace and purpose in our ministry, we must attend to the whispered appeals of the Spirit in the everyday burdens and blessings that come our way. We do not have to look far for crosses to carry. They present themselves in the most ordinary exercises of ministry like trying to devise the agenda for a meeting. Life flows along rather unreflectively until some stressful demand breaks into our routine and reminds us not to take God's presence for granted. Even when the goals we set have been achieved, they remain empty if we do not pay attention to the meaning the mystery wants to convey through us. Approaching our ministry with a humble heart facilitates our ability to disclose the divine directives embedded in the ups and downs of each ministerial situation.

No intricate schemes we devise can capture this inspiration. The more anxiously we pursue success and notoriety, the more obscure the path to self-giving love and service becomes. We are like people climbing the stairs of a tower with a millstone around our neck.

To foster appreciative living in the Lord, we must give up our demanding ways and take delight in a more gentle life style. It creates an atmosphere in which we become attuned to the Divine Source of all that is. Under stress we fail to hear what life might be telling us. We are out of touch with the thoughts, feelings, and hopes expressed by others. By contrast, when appreciation prevails, we entrust to God circumstances beyond our control. Every episode of tension contains its own challenges. None is a mere repetition of formerly workable or unworkable solutions.

Appreciation sparks creativity. It tempers ingrained prejudices and breaks through the shell of our secret indifference. It silences our feeling of being intimidated by popular pulsations or peer pressures that run contrary to God's will.

Such a delicate balance between blessings and burdens is not easy to obtain. Our perceptions are clouded by expectations and ambitions that block our vision of God's tender mercy, but it is never too late to change. Having reached this decisive transition point from distress to normal stress, we may become living witnesses to the truth that in every obstacle there resides a formation opportunity. The saintly priest, Charles de Foucald, captures in this oft-quoted prayer of his our heartfelt conviction that if God is with us, who can be against us?

> Father,
> I abandon myself into your hands;
> do with me what you will.
> Whatever you may do, I thank you:
> I am ready for all, I accept all.
> Let only your will be done in me,
> and in all your creatures.
> I wish no more than this, O Lord.
> Into your hands I commend my soul;
> I offer it to you with all the love of my heart,
> for I love you Lord, and so need to give myself,
> to surrender myself into your hands, without reserve
> and with boundless confidence,
> for you are my Father.

## *Questions for Reflection*

1. Can you name a passage from Holy Scripture or a spiritual classic that addresses your hunger to be granted by grace an appreciative heart? What effect does this inspiration have on you?

**Your Thoughts:**

2. How might your life change if you gave thanks for everything from the smallest accomplishment to the grandest success?

**Your Thoughts:**

3. When you stop to appreciate all that is as a gift of God; how is this enlightened viewing connected with the three infused virtues of faith, hope, and love?

**Your Thoughts:**

4. What does it take to live in appreciative abandonment to the mystery in the face of a personal or communal crisis in your current ministry?

**Your Thoughts:**

5. Having let go of the expectations of how your formation story "should" have been written, how have you come to accept "what is" as God's gift?

**Your Thoughts:**

## Scripture Meditations

**Psalm 126:2-4**

> When the LORD brought home the captives to
>     Zion,
>     we seemed to be dreaming.
> Our mouths were filled with laughter
>     and our tongues with songs of joy.
>
> Then it was said among the nations,
>     "The LORD has done great things for them."
> The LORD has indeed done great deeds for us,
>     and we are overflowing with joy.
>
> Once again restore our fortunes, O LORD,
>     as you did for the streams in the Negeb.

**Acts 5:12-16**

Now many signs and wonders were done among the people through the apostles. And they were all together in Solomon's Portico. None of the rest dared to join them, but the people held them in high esteem. Yet more than ever believers were added to the Lord, great numbers of both men and women, so that they even carried out the sick into the streets, and laid them on cots and mats, in order that Peter's shadow might fall on some of them as he came by. A great number of people would also gather from the towns around Jerusalem, bringing the sick and those tormented by unclean spirits, and they were all cured.

### *Meditative Exercises*

1. What glad tidings is the Lord offering to your life these days?

**Your Thoughts:**

2. If you are being called by God to be a healing presence, what can you do to help others proclaim the blessings in every burden?

**Your Thoughts:**

# 4

# Becoming Ministers of Christian Joy

*When I feel lonely, forgotten, rejected, or despised, I can easily be tempted to respond to these painful experiences with anger, resentment, and a desire for revenge. Much violence in our world is a desperate acting-out of that wounded inner self. But if I am willing to claim my woundedness as a unique way to the resurrection, then I may start caring for my wounds, knowing that they will identify me in my eternal life in God. What does this "caring for my wounds" mean? It means acknowledging them as revelations of my unique way of being human, listening to them as teachers who help me find my own way to holiness, sharing them as a source of consolation and comfort, and allowing others to pour oil on them and bind them in times of great pain.*

*Thus I proclaim that my wounds are not causes for embarrassment, but the source of a joyful acknowledgment of my unique vocation to journey with Jesus through suffering to the glory of God.*

—Henri J. M. Nouwen

Concern for growing through the stress of ministry should not dim our joyfulness nor obfuscate the necessity of restoring Christian love and concern in typically tense, joyless situations of labor and leisure. The life of the spirit is a journey to freedom in the Lord. Among its chief characteristics are spontaneity and playfulness. To link ministerial maturation with joyfulness counteracts the tendency to consider growing in Christ grim and serious business, demanding rigid discipline and proofs of functionalistic accomplishments. Such a vision of spiritual and social advancement tends to suppress ready laughter, needed rest and relaxation. The art of joyful living risks becoming the most neglected art of all. Joy ought not to be a rare, private occurrence but a way of flowing with grace and growing through the stress of ministry in the public sphere.

The bubbling up of joy may strike us as a childish outburst. After all, isn't it our duty to whip ourselves and others into shape? This frivolity might weaken the nuts and bolts business of becoming a responsible citizen in a progressive society where wasting time for play and prayer seems almost sinful. The opposite is true. Sharing our joy with others is the Christian thing to do. It prevents us from falling into a posture of superficial glee that resists giving glory to God by means of showing sincere signs of care and genuinely rejoicing in the Lord.

### Necessity of Joy

Joy is a spontaneous expression of our relaxed receptivity to a transcendent mystery in whose benevolence we deeply believe and for whose mercy we endlessly hope. Absence of exhausting overwork releases the potency for joy at the center of our redeemed existence. This disposition swells our heart with love; it attracts us to goodness, truth, and beauty. It liberates us from anxious concerns because we are content to be present where we are.

Observe the joy in infants whose parents show them all the love and care they crave. Smiles and laughter abound. When first words are spoken in a playful fashion, the joy of performance lights up a child's face. It spreads sunshine around them and melts the clouds of sadness away. Joy is contagious. It enhances everyone's health and wellbeing.

In the stressful ministerial situations in which we find ourselves as adults, we need to return to this pristine time of original delight. Although our daily experiences are not always pleasant, we can cope with them more joyfully when we operate from a transcendent perspective. On this plane true joy can be found. What is no longer gratifying on the vital level or satisfying in the functional realm may still turn into an occasion to rejoice. Picture our Lord on the cross. All pleasures and displeasures, all satisfactions and dissatisfactions disappeared. All that remained was the joy of redemption that pierced the heavens and transformed the earth.

This paradox of joy in sorrow can best be seen in the lives of the holy martyrs. In the face of pain and persecution, of death and destruction, they remembered the words of the psalmist:

> But may all who take refuge in you rejoice;
>     may they shout for joy forever.
> Grant them your protection
> so that those who love your name may rejoice
>     in you.
> Truly, you bless the righteous, O LORD;
>     you surround them with your goodwill as
>     with a shield.
>                                        (Psalm 5:12-13)

There is no use denying how much adversity disturbs us. Our ministry often exhausts us. The wear and tear of daily living costs us dearly. Yet the more we strive to read disconcerting facts as invitations to deeper faith, the more we see the light of joy radiating from within them. Affliction advances our flight to freedom.

We need to be more like good parents, who do not waste time complaining about the unpleasant stresses that accompany child rearing like diaper changing, meal preparation, and laundry duty. One smile from their little one seems to make heavy chores light. They have found from experience that nurturing the soul of others is the essence of ministry and the best destressor anyone could hope to find.

## Art of Joyful Living

Our technological society promises us more leisure time, but do we really believe in the truth of this claim? Stress-related illnesses, far from being on the decline, are on the rise. Advertisements for one drug after the other fill the air waves. Quick psychological fixes are promoted as common fare, even if their effects have no staying power. A worry we all share concerns the question of how we can regain some balance in our lives.

Our walk with Christ through the pains and joys of ministry convinces us that the first step to becoming spiritually mature is to contemplate with joy God's sustaining presence in our lives at every moment. As souls redeemed by Christ we echo the psalmist's words, "Even though I walk through the darkest valley, I fear no evil" (Psalm 23:4). The joy we feel, even when death itself stalks at our door, is only understandable in the light of what the Lord told us: "I came that [you] may have life, and have it abundantly" (John 10:10).

The freedom of the children of God is a participation in the essence of divine joyfulness. Swamped though we may be by stresses of every sort, we try to read every chapter of our formation story as a rendition of these words of wisdom and joy presented so vividly in the Book of Proverbs:

> When he established the heavens, I was there,
> when he drew a circle on the face of the deep,
> when he made firm the skies above,
> when he established the fountains of the deep,
> when he assigned to the sea its limit,
> so that the waters might not transgress his command,
> when he marked out the foundations of the earth,
> then I was beside him, like a master worker;
> and I was daily his delight,
>     rejoicing before him always,
> rejoicing in his inhabited world
>     and delighting in the human race.
>
> (Proverbs 8:27-31)

Such joyousness reverberates through our whole being and gives us a share in God's eternal delight. In the midst of earthly concerns, we find sweet consolation. Morose ministers may get a task done, but no one around them sees much evidence of the Good News. As joyful laborers in the vineyard of the Lord, we try to strike a happy mean between being uproariously funny clowns or somber souls who find it hard to smile.

Different from raucous humor or silly joking is the relaxed ability to point to the goodness we see around us, no matter how tense a situation may be. This arena of appreciation is the place where wisdom builds her house (cf. Proverbs 9:1). In its corridors the sharp edges of stress are tempered by the soothing music of eternity. One who embraces the joy of wise living knows that its ways are "paths of peace." Wisdom is " . . . a tree of life to those who lay hold of her; those who hold her fast are called happy" (Proverbs 3:17-18).

Formation in joyousness is a healing necessity in our era. Far too many of us are trapped in stressful functionalism. It kills mirth and casts us into the barren desert of calculative control at the expense of other people.

One of the best ways to cope with the stress of ministry is to bear patiently with the disappointments of daily life. When our heart is light, when we are not burdened by the weight of the world, our life becomes more carefree without losing the capacity to be caring. We continue our journey with the easy step of one who is no longer bending under heavy loads. Our life in time reflects the wisdom of eternity. We catch ourselves more readily when we lose joy and start to trudge through this world like troops of ants. One member of the colony cannot be distinguished from the next. All of them follow the same functional line until they die. Such stressed out seriousness is reason enough to bring us to our knees in prayer. *Father, Son, and Holy Spirit, give us the saving grace of joyful living. There is no chance for us to gain it on our own. Please relieve us from the stress of relentless labor. Teach us the sweet marvel of wasting time in leisurely contemplation. Amen.*

**Sharing Our Joy with Others**

As companions of Christ in this world, we see our ministry as an opportunity to share his joy with all sincerely seeking souls: with the sick of body, mind, and spirit, with victims of injustice and survivors of debilitating disrespect, disinterest, and outright indifference. We know from experience that joyless judgmentalism paralyzes Christian presence and action. Christ himself said, "Go and learn what this means, 'I desire mercy, not sacrifice.' For I have come to call not the righteous but sinners" (Matthew 9:13).

The more we allow the joyful Christ to guide us, the more we feel our ministry being released from the burdens of utilitarian pressures and chronological intensity. We are not naive people. We realize that joyful living requires taking a risk. What if the kindness we bestow on others is not shown to us in return? Do we grow hard of heart or treat such disappointments as humorous reminders of the human condition? What we choose to focus on is the fact that the "steadfast love of the Lord endures forever and that his joy, like his mercy, extends "from everlasting to everlasting" to those who live in awe of him (cf. Psalm 103:17).

Such joyful love can only flow through us to others if we remember our kinship in the Body of Christ. As members of the family of God, we are . . . one in Christ Jesus" (cf. Galatians 3:28). He lifts us beyond the crushing weight of human cruelty and joyless indifference and teaches us to draw our strength for ministry from his saving compassion. We may be mocked as fools for trying to imitate his healing presence, but we choose to persevere in our mission.

Joy enables us to see behind finite failings the infinite worth of each person. We sense with glee how alike we are. A marvelous model of what it means to be a minister of Christian joy is Saint Thérèse of Lisieux. In her autobiography, *The Story of a Soul*, she gives us a stunning example of what joyful service in the Lord really asks of us:

One winter night I was carrying out my little duty as usual; it was cold, it was night. Suddenly, I heard off in the distance the harmonious sound of a musical instrument. I then pictured a well-lighted drawing room brilliantly gilded, filled with elegantly dressed young ladies conversing together and conferring upon each other all sorts of compliments and other worldly remarks. Then my glance fell upon the poor invalid whom I was supporting. Instead of the beautiful strains of music I heard only her occasional complaints, and instead of the rich gildings I saw only the bricks of our austere cloister, hardly visible in the faintly glimmering light. I cannot express in words what happened in my soul; what I know is that the Lord illumined it with rays of *truth* which so surpassed the dark brilliance of earthly feasts that I could not believe my happiness. Ah! I would not have exchanged the ten minutes employed in carrying out my humble office of charity to enjoy a thousand years of worldly feasts. If already in suffering and in combat one can enjoy a moment of happiness that surpasses all the joys of this earth, and this when simply considering that God has withdrawn us from this world, what will this happiness be in heaven when one shall see in the midst of the eternal joy of everlasting repose the incomparable grace the Lord gave us when he chose to *dwell in his house*, heaven's real portal?

## Praying for Peace and Joy

As the Farewell Discourse in the Gospel of John suggests, joy is inseparable from peace. To his beloved apostles Christ says, "Peace I leave with you; my peace I give to you" (John 14:27). To grow through the stress of ministry is to become living witnesses to Christian peace and joy. This pledge places a new challenge before us.

Picture a pond in winter. A skater pivoting on the ice. A solitary person day after day practicing a figure-eight. Turn, reverse, turn–climaxing in a vigorous yet graceful spin. The secret of such a feat is the skater's ability to focus on one object. As long as he or she concentrates on a tree, a fence, a point on the distant horizon, loss of balance is less likely to occur. As the skater's calm performance is not disrupted by the whirlwind activity around the pond, so we need a core of inner peace enabling us to act from the center of our integrative heart.

The demands of our professional life can result in abnormal levels of stress. The tension of nervous strain affects us. We run out of energy. We lose track of the direction our life ought to take. Now is the time not to keep spinning but to ask ourselves if we have lost the ultimate "for what" of our ministry.

To maintain inner peace for the sake of outer effectiveness we have to fix our gaze on Christ, the axis and compass of our endeavors. We need to gather together the circles of activity in which we feel ourselves becoming dispersed. We have to look at our involvements and discern which have the most priority in response to the love-will of the Trinity. For the sake of inner calm, we must let go of peripheral concerns.

The cause of our agitation is most frequently a shift from the Divine Forming Mystery at the center of our field of life to our own isolated ego, which is adept at "Easing God Out." To be at peace and to live in joy, we must be convinced that our restlessness can only be laid to rest when we surrender our will over a lifetime to our Lord.

A friend of ours lost her mother after a long, painful illness. Though she felt daily the stress and strain of nursing her aged mother, she accepted to be her caregiver with quiet devotion. After her mother died, she was for others a model of serenity. When her friends asked what had happened to her, she simply said:

> I learned not to seek for the answer as to why mother had to suffer so much but to ask only for trust and

strength. When the pressures got to be too much to bear and there was no where else to turn, I cried out in my desperation for divine help. The peace I felt was God's reply. It was not mine to give.

This good woman knew that she could not wish away the stress such a ministry placed upon her. Demanding work takes its toll on us. In the midst of stress this intense, we have no choice but to bring our worn out selves at the end of each day before the altar of the Lord. We pray to find comfort in the words of Holy Scripture:

> "Therefore do not worry, saying, 'What will we eat?' or 'What will we drink?' or 'What will we wear?' For it is the Gentiles who strive for all these things; and indeed your heavenly Father knows that you need all these things. But strive first for the kingdom of God and his righteousness, and all these things will be given to you as well.
>
> "So do not worry about tomorrow, for tomorrow will bring worries of its own. Today's trouble is enough for today." (Matthew 6:31-34)

### Be Still and Know that I am God! (Psalm 46:10)

On some days our stress is so intense that it takes a while for us to come to rest in the Lord. We may need to listen to music, to sit and talk with a friend, to seek solace in nature. Such nonstressful moments restore our spirit. They are not a luxury for the spiritually elite but a survival measure for all.

When we dwell with the Trinity in recollected presence, we do not engage in a magic act that makes the pressures associated with our ministry instantly disappear, but we do start to regain our equanimity. Our problems may not be solved as quickly as we would like, but at least we find the link between our humility and God's will.

Perhaps the image of a revolving cartwheel might serve as an appropriate illustration of this reunion. When we watch the wheel turn slowly, we see that the hub is the axis around which everything rotates. As it gathers speed, all the activity seems to move from the center towards the periphery. At first glance it appears as if the movements at the fringe of the wheel are isolated from the rest of the mechanism. A closer look shows that it is the hub that keeps the whole wheel rotating and gaining more speed.

Our inner core of peace is like the center point of this wheel. It reminds us that we can only carry on if we do not become separated from our center in God. This still point in the depths of our soul is not a physical place but a spiritual refuge. Amidst the tumult of any serious task, we can retire to the hermitage of our heart and regain our strength.

What Christ promised us was not peace without tension but peace that would endure regardless of surface disruptions. In the light of this promise, we can perceive dissonance as a call to deeper consonance with his suffering, death, and resurrection. We may not understand all that Christ asks of us in the throes of ministerial distress, but we can open our heart to him and allow his mercy to filter through our most anxious concerns.

Often it feels as if we are no more than wind-tossed reeds. Along the riverbank of life, we are cast hither and yon by storms that sometimes flatten us to the ground. When the fury of the wind subsides and we stroll by water's edge, we are amazed at the resilience fragile reeds display. There they are, upright and perfect in the morning breeze. How can a reed bend so low and yet refuse to break? Is it not because far below the surface of the ground, in the silent depths of its roots, it has dug itself into the bedrock soil of the marshland from whence it finds the strength to bend but not break.

Our challenge is to do the same. There are moments in ministry when our superiors are rudely demanding, our colleagues enviously competitive, our recipients of care ungrateful. Our best efforts seem to be in vain. We feel miserable in the face of defeat, hurt by a lack of understanding, leveled like reeds by forces that threaten us on all sides. We become harsh with ourselves and others. We want to whip such lackadaisical lives into shape, but all we succeed in doing is becoming more depreciated.

Caught in the net of such stressful entrapments, we might recall that passage from Holy Scripture that describes the apostles as so fearful of sinking one stormy night they awakened the Master, who instantly calmed the waves. He quieted their fears and then reprimanded them for their lack of faith (cf. Mark 4:35-41). He wanted them to stand tall and erect like reeds after a storm, at peace with themselves, with others, and with the whole cosmos. Being worry-free enkindled in them a readiness to reach out to others and be of service to them.

It is difficult to descend into the spiritual center of our soul if fear dominates our lives. Since "perfect love casts out fear" (1 John 4:18), it enables us to replace abnormal distress with normal stress. In the stillness that surrounds us, our muscles relax. Our minds are free of preoccupying thoughts. Our spirit rests in God. Slowly it dawns on us that our ministry is not the same. All that we do has been transformed by an infinite peace and joy words alone fail to comprehend. We listen with a happy smile to the counsels given by the Apostle Paul to those he has commissioned to be messengers of the mystery:

> Rejoice in the Lord always; again I will say, Rejoice.
> Let your gentleness be known to everyone. The Lord
> is near. Do not worry about anything, but in every-
> thing by prayer and supplication with thanksgiving
> let your requests be made known to God. And the
> peace of God, which surpasses all understanding,
> will guard your hearts and your minds in Christ
> Jesus.                                    (Philippians 4:4-7)

### Questions for Reflection

1.  Do you remember to pray daily for the gifts of peace and joy? Why are these the main marks of growing in spiritual maturity in imitation of Christ?

**Your Thoughts:**

2.  Give a concrete example of how you maintain the disposition of joyousness amidst the trials of daily ministry? How do you renew this gift when it starts to wane?

**Your Thoughts:**

3.  Do you find yourself becoming more sensitive to what Christ would want you to do as a bearer of the Good News, especially in situations where animosity prevails.

**Your Thoughts:**

4.  How would you articulate the connection between diminishing stress and heightening the wisdom of joyfulness? What lasting dispositions of the heart light up this path to peace?

**Your Thoughts:**

5.  Give a few examples of ways to live with the disappointments to be found in every ministerial situation without losing your peace and joy. How would you teach others, young and old, to emulate "the joy of the Lord [which] is your strength" (Nehemiah 8:10)?

**Your Thoughts:**

## Scripture Meditations

**Psalm 16:9-11:**

> Therefore, my heart is glad
>    and my soul rejoices;
>    my body too is filled with confidence.
> For you will not abandon me to the nether-
>    world
>    or allow your Holy One to suffer corrup-
>    tion.
>
> You will show me the path to life;
>    you will fill me with joy in your presence
>    and everlasting delights at your right hand.

**Luke 18:18-23:**

A certain ruler asked him, "Good Teacher, what must I do to inherit eternal life?" Jesus said to him, "Why do you call me good? No one is good but God alone. You know the commandments: 'You shall not commit adultery; You shall not shall not steal; You shall not bear false witness; Honor your father and mother.'" He replied, "I have kept all these since my youth." When Jesus heard this, he said to him, "There is still one thing lacking. Sell all that you own and distribute the money to the poor, and you will have treasure in heaven; then come, follow me." But when he heard this, he became sad; for he was very rich.

*Meditative Exercises*

1. Why did the rich young man in this parable go away sad? What eroded and depleted his sense of joy? How do you think it can be recovered?

**Your Thoughts:**

2. What do these texts say to you about living more holistically in and with the Lord and about seeing his peace and joy as the surest signs of effective ministerial presence?

**Your Thoughts:**

# 5

# Turning from the Dissonance of Stress to the Consonance of True Happiness

*The happenings at the Synod have been a great spiritual experience for all the participants. The experience has been that of a Church under the light and the power of the Spirit, intent on discerning and embracing the renewed call of her Lord so that she can again propose to today's world, the mystery of her communion and the dynamism of her mission of salvation, especially, by centering on the specific place and role of the lay faithful. This exhortation* (Christifidelis Laici) *then intends to urge the most abundant possible fruitfulness from this Synod in every part of the Church worldwide. This will come about as a result of an effective hearkening to the Lord's call by the entire People of God, in particular, by the lay faithful.*

—Pope John Paul II

Grappling with the dissonance of stress before it spoils our happiness is perhaps the most important task of Christian ministry. Living with less stress and more confidence in Christ is an ideal worthy to pursue. The remedy we choose to relieve tension is not a fake smile or a cheap joke or a binging-out experience, but the pursuit of intimacy with the Lord. We try not to succumb to the temptation to let "administration" take precedence over "ministry." We see that our ministry suffers most when we lack compassion. However technically competent we may be, it is difficult to dislodge others' perception of us as cold, calculative, uncongenial managers, dedicated more to institutional order than to the people our institutions ought to embrace and serve. Legalistic approaches to every problem banish trust and compatibility, two ingredients of productive teamwork. The opposite dispositions need to be put into place.

*Congeniality* means to respect the original, unrepeatable uniqueness of self and others. We strive gently and firmly to nurture our own and their unique-communal call in Christ. When we confirm one another's true originality and its Sacred Origin, we are drawn into a circle of care that is life-giving.

*Compatibility* means that we must meet the demands of everyday ministerial situations with patience and prudence, avoiding any semblance of disrespect for others' gifts and limits. To maintain a caring presence in the midst of trying moments, we also need to exercise a certain amount of flexibility. The more compatible our presence is, the better we may be able to plant the seeds of Christ's peace in the hearts and minds of all who cross our path.

To be *compassionate* means that we remain sensitive to our own and others' vulnerability. We try not to mix up practical and ultimate judgments. We stand ready to love and forgive the sinner while hating the sin. Such compassionate care does not emanate from ourselves alone; it is a gift granted to us through the power of the Holy Spirit.

To be *competent* means to pursue the wisdom, knowledge, and skills required for effective ministry. Our goal is not to become "managerial robots" but "epiphanic manifestations" of Divine Mercy. To hear, obey, and embody the teachings of Christ is to point others towards that for which they hunger and thirst, often without their knowing it. To be most competent is to remember that we are only servants who beg the Lord to give us listening ears (cf. Matthew 11:15).

To implement congenial, compatible, compassionate, competent service in Christ's name requires courage, the virtue that enables us to persevere despite the stressful obstacles strewn on our path, and candor, the virtue that signifies the capacity to be honest with ourselves, others, and God.

To radiate the glory of the Lord, we need to cultivate the seeds of these dispositions in such good soil that they bloom in society as a whole. All four of them as virtues of the Christian heart correspond to the societal virtues of justice, peace, mercy, and action.

Our concern to provide optimal conditions for the congenial unfolding of people in all walks of life gives rise to social justice. It preserves the right every person has to pursue his or her congenial life call and to do so within the context of given and chosen vocations and avocations.

The disposition of compatibility supports our intention to promote social peace and harmony among the children of God. As brothers and sisters adopted into the family of the Trinity, we must try to encourage the pursuit of non-violent dialogue and pave the way to world peace by first making peace around our own kitchen table.

The core disposition of compassion opens our arms to others in social mercy. Gross instances of inhumanity from starving the poor to feed the rich, from imprisoning the innocent to assure a place for the powerful, signify how wide the reach of human and divine mercy must be.

Competence in ministry gives rise to specific actions that address the demands of justice, peace, and mercy in fidelity to God's loving plan for all people. Christ wants us to heed his words in the most responsible way our ministry allows: "Amen, I say to you, whatever you did for one of these least brothers [and sisters] of mine, you did for me" (Matthew 25:40).

When it feels as if everything we touch turns to failure, we need to look to the Lord for comfort. He had to deal with countless disappointments, with loyal friends who became betrayers, with an occasional victory, as in the case of Nicodemus (cf. John 3:1-21), and many more defeats as when ten lepers were cleansed but only one returned to thank him (cf. Luke 17:11-19).

So much did he trust his Father's will that no instance of stress could retard the mission he intended to fulfill, even to the point of "death on a cross" (Philippians 2:8).

If our ministry fails it is not because of a lack of grace. Divine direction disclosures are revealed through our daily circumstances, no matter how trivial they may seem. Instead of cooperating with God's plan, we may have insisted on being in control. We opted for overexertion, undue speed, and ego exaltation rather than being content, in the words of Mother Teresa of Calcutta, to be little pens in a Mighty Hand.

## Acting Appropriately

Once we see the life situations in which we find ourselves in an epiphanic light, we experience a softening of the hard edges of stress. We feel more relaxed as soon as we pause to assess what ails us from a spiritual perspective. The dissonance caused by willful impatience diminishes our effectiveness. By contrast, our consonant presence to divinely initiated invitations, challenges, and appeals shows us what needs to be done. More room is left for the Spirit to enlighten us. If anything, we gain in graciousness and act more appropriately.

A contemplative orientation relieves us from too much inward concentration and the torment of incessant self-examination. Surrender with the Son to the Father removes what triggers stress. We no longer feel obliged to keep up pretenses or to worry ourselves to death over what others may say or think about us.

## Flowing with the Graces in Every Situation

When coercive directives rule our ministry, we want to grasp at success as swiftly as possible. We become impatient with ourselves and others, anxiously pursuing goals that yield honors and privileges at the expense of other people's needs. Under such circumstances, we find neither peace of heart nor the motivation for wholehearted commitment. We start from a false image of self that distorts our perception of the situation.

To flow with what is as a source of life directives, is to give up "control center me" and the scrupulous distrust that compels us to check up on everyone else's thoughts, feelings, and actions. When we habitually do our best in response to grace, we are less likely to fret about failure. We are no longer swept up in a whirlwind of stress. With our feet planted firmly on a plateau of transcendent freedom, we see points of tension as lovely facets of the diamond of our spiritual direction.

This quiet flowing with the grace of every situation does not have to be felt. It is a way of sharing in Christ's obedience to whatever the Father allowed to happen during his life and now by extension our own. The medieval master, Johannes Tauler, tells us from whence this meaning flows, saying:

> In these heavenly hollows
> the soul finds all its good,
> for there dwells all divine joys.
> In them the soul is still,
> centered in God
> and drawn into uncreated
> bliss.
> This is God, acting, dwelling, ruling, granting the soul
> the gift of Divine life.
> Into this life the soul melts
> away
> into the endless light and fire
> of love that God is
> by essence and nature.

Mere functionality, in contrast to flowing with grace, forces us to forge an isolated ego-identity, marked by complacent self-importance and condescending arrogance. It thrives on envious competition, not on compatibility and compassion, and surely not on obedient congeniality with the mystery at the center of our life.

Since the Fall, we are inclined to be imprisoned by our self-centeredness and the pride-form on which it feeds. This bent towards functionalism and vitalism can be a source of high stress. To overcome it calls for a total conversion of heart. Lying in wait for our consent are the virtues of congeniality, compatibility, compassion, and competence. They are reservoirs of grace since the mystery itself is endlessly congenial; utterly compatible with its manifestations in cosmos and humanity; compassionate with all kinds of suffering; and everlastingly competent and all-powerful.

No one can relieve all the needs of doers and seekers in different walks of life. Every ministry must be balanced by *obedient congeniality,* meaning that we must listen to (obedience) our uniqueness and be at home with our limits and our gifts (congeniality). Compassion must not become an excuse for disregarding those who are not visibly suffering. They still need our sympathy. Always welcome are *patient expressions of compatibility* like not pushing people, especially the elderly, to hurry up because we have to get somewhere on time. The virtue of patience makes us more compatible or at home with the needs of others. When competence complements this triad of transcendent dispositions, our heart experiences an oasis of consonance together with a deepening of faith, hope, and love. Our primary stance in life should not be based on any one of these virtues, but on the rhythmic flow and graceful modulation of them all.

## Living with Less Stress and More Confidence

When we learn to rely on God totally, our stress lessens and our confidence increases. In every conflict we seek for ways to consecrate our life anew with Christ to the Father. The bread of our daily responsibility and the wine of our suffering are transformed through the power of the Spirit into the Eucharist of everydayness. To partake of it is to go where God wants to lead us and to see ourselves simply as sojourners on this sacred road. At times we travel in fear and trembling towards our goal of union with God for the sake of serving others. We rely for guidance on the guiding words and deeds of people who have gone before us as well as on those most near to us. Anyone in ministry not open to the counsel of more experienced people lives to regret it. Without humility, the wisdom of experience eludes us.

Once in a while we know with surprising clarity what God asks of us, despite the stress it may entail. It takes time to become aware of the depth dimension of our call because we are free to accept or refuse that to which we are being led. God does not force a response. Neither can we predict the way we ought to go nor the kind of guidance we need to get there. Our task is to trust. Even if we fail to overcome the obstacles strewn before us, we are confident that in some way God will bring good out of our less than perfect attempts to grow through the stress of ministry.

## Questions for Reflection

1. Give a concrete example of how you have shown concern for people in your particular ministerial setting. Was it during a casual conversation or while planning a program and trying to rally support for some new ideas? Do you humbly consult with people in authority as the need arises?

**Your Thoughts:**

2. When was the last time you remember offering others verbal or nonverbal expressions of assurance, appreciation, and encouragement? How did your confirmation help them to affirm themselves?

**Your Thoughts:**

3. Why is a commitment to cooperation so significant in every ministerial situation? What in your experience most hinders and what most helps people in such a setting to work together to serve the common good?

**Your Thoughts:**

4.  Do you plan regular occasions to "concelebrate" each person's unique gifts, talents, and achievements? Why is having fun together as a faith community so important? What uplifts and what drags down the morale of people who must become partners in the mystery of redemption?

**Your Thoughts:**

5.  Have you taken time lately, in prayer and appraisal before the Lord, to reaffirm the pursuit of ministerial and professional excellence to the best of your ability?

**Your Thoughts:**

## *Scripture Meditations*

### 1 John 2:24-29

Let what you heard from the beginning abide in you. If what you heard from the beginning abides in you, then you will abide in the Son and in the Father. And this is what he has promised us, eternal life. I write these things to you concerning those who would deceive you. As for you, the anointing that you received from him abides in you, and so you do not need anyone to teach you. But as his anointing teaches you about all things, and is true and is not a lie, and just as it has taught you, abide in him. And now, little children, abide in him, so that when he is revealed we may have confidence and not be put to shame before him at his coming. If you know that he is righteous, you may be sure that everyone who does right has been born of him.

### 1 Peter 1:13-16

Therefore prepare your minds for action; discipline yourselves; set all your hope on the grace that Jesus Christ will bring you when he is revealed. Like obedient children, do not be conformed to the desires that you formerly had in ignorance. Instead, as he who called you is holy, be holy yourselves in all your conduct; for it is written, "You shall be holy, for I am holy."

## *Meditative Exercises*

1. How do these passages from John and Peter suggest ways of modeling your ministry on the mystery of the Trinity?

**Your Thoughts:**

2. How would you describe the link between the universal call to holiness and the art and discipline of living holistically? What effect does this connection have on helping you to grow more holy and happy under stress?

**Your Thoughts:**

# Afterword

Whatever our mode of ministerial presence may be, Christ is our model of what it means to meet people where they are and to serve them in ways consonant with our calling in him. He reminds us that periods of pondering our destiny in the desert are as necessary for ministry as deeper communion with the people for whom we care. This rhythm of solitude and solidarity, of contemplation and action, is an essential part of Christian ministry. Which one of these orientations will be more prevalent depends on the needs set before us, on the direction the Spirit inspires us to follow and on the formation phase in which we find ourselves.

For example, contemplative monks bridge the gap between monastic living and worldly needs by their ministry of prayer and work. Mothers and fathers witness to another way of incorporating daily prayer into the myriad details demanded by the ministry of good parenting. They, too, manifest in their own simple yet profound way the meaning of the hidden life led by the Holy Family in Nazareth.

Worship and work, labor and leisure, constitute the receptive and donative components that help us to grow through the stress of ministry. With time and patience, we learn how to integrate all that we are and do in our Christ-formed heart.

For the benefit of those whom we love and serve, we contemplate what it means to be in the temple of the Lord, sensing, believing, and experiencing that he is in us and we are in him. This basic union never changes. Whatever obstacles may be strewn on the contemplative-active path we are to follow, Christ is with us and for us, however lost and confused we may feel.

Silence, spiritual reading, meditation, and prayer assure the priority we give to a life of worshipful presence and diligent service. Stress lessens when we see the little we can accomplish in the light of the divine plan for our lives. Through stillness and listening, reflection and receptivity, we appraise and act upon the directives disclosed to us by the Spirit in our daily situation. These spiritual disciplines, faithfully practiced, prepare us to handle ministerial upheavals without losing either our peace or our joy.

To ready us for transformation in Christ, what has to die is not our deepest self, our being made in the form and likeness of God (cf. Genesis 1:26-27), but the illusion that our functional ego is all-powerful. Once we shed the imprisoning restrictions of self-centeredness and acknowledge anew our dependency on God, we are free to serve others with compassion and Christian excellence, caring for all abandoned souls as our Beloved cares for us.

The ebb and flow of contemplative ministry and ministerial contemplation involve the slow relinquishing over a lifetime of the selfish desires that stand between us and full surrender to God. They are what make us tense and unhappy. Every time we separate prayer and participation stress is the result. We need both of these wings of ministry, operating at full power, to experience the sheer joy of soaring freely, without distress, to that place where Christ calls us to serve in his name.

At certain moments, we may sense in a manner completely unexpected that the living God has drawn us to himself in an embrace of love that is almost overwhelming. The wound that burned during sensual and spiritual purification is suddenly sweet; the fire that consumed is soothingly benevolent. This experience propels us to a new depth of commitment to live contemplatively and to serve tirelessly, to blend fidelity pauses with zealous perseverance. To grow through the stress of ministry is to move from silent awe to creative articulation of our call to model uniquely and communally Christ's way of responding to the needs of our world.

This rhythm of adoration and action is an essential feature of Christian ministry. Whatever we do—be it cooking a meal, writing a letter, teaching a class, or nursing the sick—we are to give of ourselves out of love for God. Making this love manifest is the best way to diminish our stress.

Ministerial excellence cannot be confined to high level appointments or missionary endeavors. It has as much, if not more, to do with fulfilling our Christian duty as joyously as possible in our homes and professions every day of our lives. To remain faithful disciples amidst the upheavals of ordinary ministry, we seek from God's treasury of grace the courage to begin each day with fresh faith, radiant hope, and tireless love. Despite the stresses that accompany the cross of Christian ministry, we can always find relief in prayer. Imprinted on our hearts may be life-giving words that prevent stress from escalating as soon as we pause to pray:

> *Let me dwell daily in your love,*
> *Let it give form to my unfolding.*
> *Let me no longer be the lonely shepherd of my life.*
> *Bring me home from the bracing highlands of the mind,*
> *From the dead end streets in which I shiver in despair.*
> *Shelter my soul tenderly when disappointment hems me in.*
> *Do not allow my soul to grow ponderous and bleak,*
> *Keep alive in me a glimmer of your joy,*
> *Let no adversity defer my course,*
> *Nor defeat my slow advance.*
> *Put a spring in my step, a smile in my heart.*
> *Let me spend this life lightheartedly.*
> *Fill it with verve and inspiration.*
> *Ploughing, we praise; sailing, we sing,*
> *To land on the shore*
> *That teems with your presence.*

—Susan Muto and Adrian van Kaam

# Prayer Service

## I. CALL TO PRAYER

Almighty and ever glorious God, you govern us with unfailing wisdom and surround us with compassionate love and care. Increase our faith and hope in you, teach us to cherish the gifts that surround us, and bring our trust to its promised fulfillment in the joy and peace of your eternal reign. We make this prayer in the name of Jesus, our Savior. Amen.

## II. SCRIPTURE MEDITATION: THE JOY OF BEING FORGIVEN

### Psalm 32

**L.** Blessed is the one whose offense is forgiven,
whose sin is erased.
Blessed is the one to whom the Lord charges no guilt
and in whose spirit there is no guile.

**R.** As long as I remained silent,
my body wasted away
as the result of my groaning throughout the day.
For day and night
your hand was heavy upon me;
my strength withered steadily
as though consumed by the summer heat.

**L.** Then I acknowledged my sin to you,
and I made no attempt to conceal my guilt.
I said, "I will confess my offenses to the Lord,"
and you removed the guilt of my sin.

**R.** Therefore, let everyone who is faithful pray to you
where you may be found.
Even if great floods threaten,
they will never reach him.
You are a place of refuge for me;
you preserve me from trouble
and surround me with songs of deliverance. *VICTORY*

**L.** I will instruct you
and guide you in the way you should go;

~ 85 ~

I will counsel you
and keep my eyes upon
you.

R. Do not behave without
understanding
like a horse or a mule;
if its temper is not curbed
with bit and bridle,
it will not come near you.

The wicked has a multi-
tude of troubles,

but the man who trusts in
the Lord
is surrounded by kindness.

L. Be glad in the Lord and
rejoice, you righteous;
shout for joy, all you
upright of heart.Rejoice,
rejoice in the Lord,
exult, you just!

### III. BRIEF SILENCE

### IV. SHARED REFLECTION ON THE PSALM AND INTERCESSORY PRAYER

### V. Spiritual Reading

#### Follow Wherever He Leads

Was it really concern for the courageous Christians I was leaving behind that saddened me, or was it personal disappointment in having to end my first really rewarding experience as a priest, just when things seemed to be going so well? Could I imagine, was I afraid, that God had no other way to take care of his people? "So I will have him wait until I come," our Lord said to Peter, "Follow thou me." Christ had called Peter aside, but Peter was concerned about John. And now Christ, through the KGB, was calling me from Norilsk. Why should I doubt that he would provide somehow for those I was leaving behind—even as he had provided for me before I came. My first concern, instead, should be to follow wherever he led, to see his will always in the events of my life and follow it faithfully, without question or hesitation.        —Walter Ciszek, S.J.
*He Leadeth Me*

## VI. Closing Meditation

**L.** Loving Mystery, Holy Trinity,
Calling us to ministry,
Inviting us to live holistically,
Help us to form, reform, and transform
Our family and community
In faith, hope, and charity.

**R.** Send us to serve our sisters and brothers
In ministry zealously, joyfully, obediently
As we offer the witness
Of love and healing,
Of prayer and presence,
Of care and consolation
To a world in desolation,
Wounded by violence, hatred, and ill will,
Discordant in soul and body because of sin.

**L.** Father, Son, Holy Spirit,
Three in One and One in three,
Overshadow our ministry
As we gather as husbands and wives,
Fathers and mothers,
Children and elders,
Friends and relatives,
Into the caring, sharing
Arms of Jesus, our Savior,
Helping us to shoulder
The burdens and blessings we laity
Must carry daily in our ministry.

**R.** Be with us, Lord, As we read God's Word,
Distribute Holy Communion,
Communicate our tradition to youth and adults,
Facing decision-making
Taking responsibility in the Church
Responding wherever we are placed
In time and space
To souls hungering, for a world revitalized
And renewed by Christ.
For a Church recreated in his image and likeness now and for all ages to come.

**L.** Teach us, Trinity divine,
To speak with a disciple's tongue,
As we lift up for all to see the treasury
We call our faith and formation story.

**R.** Save us from lukewarmness

Or indifference so that the cry of our heart
May be a constant reminder
Of your resurrected presence everywhere.

**L.** Give us the courage to fulfill our ministry,
The confidence to care for others
As epiphanic reminders of your Mystery.
Help us to be compassionate messengers
Serving people faithfully
Despite confusing polarities.

**R.** Dearest Mary, Our Mother of mercy,
Our Lady of Epiphany,

Finest witness to what it means to live holistically.
Help us to imitate your spirit of courage and consent, of loyalty and dedication,
As we strive to shoulder the awesome responsibility the Father gave us to be
People in ministry.

**L.** Mother of our Lord, may the Word you cherished become flesh in us, as we strive to foster day by day the spiritual formation,
the radiant transformation, of all we hold dear.

**All:** In Jesus' name, though many,
In one voice we say,
Amen! Alleluia! Amen!

—Susan Muto and Adrian van Kaam

# For Further Reading

à Kempis, Thomas. *Consolations for My Soul.* Trans. William Griffin. New York, NY: Crossroad Publishing, 2004.

à Kempis, Thomas. *The Imitation of Christ.* Ed. William C. Creasy. Notre Dame, IN: Ave Maria Press, 1989.

*The Ascent of Mount Carmel* in *The Collected Works of St. John of the Cross.* Trans. Kieran Kavanaugh, O.C.D. and Otilio Rodriguez, O.C.D. Washington, DC: ICS Publications, 1991.

Brennan, Patrick J. *Re-Imagining the Parish.* New York: Crossroad, 1993.

Brother Lawrence of the Resurrection. *The Practice of the Presence of God.* Critical Edition, Conrad De Meester. Salvatore Sciurba, Trans. Washington, DC: ICS Publications, 1994.

Carretto, Carlo. *Letters from the Desert.* Trans. Rose Mary Hancock. Maryknoll, NY: Orbis Books, 1972.

*Catherine of Siena, The Dialogue.* Mahwah, NJ: Paulist Press, 1980.

*Christifideles Laici. The Vocation and the Mission of the Lay Faithful in the Church and in the World.* Washington, DC: United States Catholic Conference, 1988.

Ciszek, Walter J., with Daniel Flaherty. *He Leadeth Me.* Garden City, NY: Image Books, Doubleday, 1975.

*The Confessions of St. Augustine.* Trans. John K. Ryan. Garden City, NY: Doubleday, 1960.

Cunningham, Lawrence S. *Francis of Assisi: Performing the Gospel Life.* Grand Rapids, MI: Eerdmans, 2004.

*The Dark Night* in *The Collected Works of St. John of the Cross.* Trans. Kieran Kavanaugh, O.C.D. and Otilio Rodriguez, O.C.D. Washington, DC: ICS Publications, 1991.

de Caussade, Jean-Pierre. *Abandonment to Divine Providence.* Trans. John Beevers. Garden City, NY: Doubleday, 1975.

*Elizabeth of the Trinity. The Complete Works.* Volumes I (1984) and II (1995). Trans. Sr. Aletheia Kane. Washington, DC: ICS Publications.

Gjergji, Lush. *Mother Teresa: To Live, To Love, To Witness.* Trans. Jordan Aumann. Hyde Park, NY: New City Press, 1998.

*Julian of Norwich: Showings* in *The Classics of Western Spirituality.* New York, NY: Paulist Press, 1978.

Lorit, Sergius C. *Charles de Foucauld: The Silent Witness.* New York, NY: New City Press, 1977.

Muto, Susan. *Caring for the Caregiver.* Pittsburgh, PA: Epiphany Association, 1996.

_____. *Celebrating the Single Life: A Spirituality for Single Persons in Today's World.* Bombay, India: St. Paul's, 1995.

_____. *John of the Cross for Today: The Ascent.* Pittsburgh, PA: Epiphany Books, 1998.

_____. *John of the Cross for Today: The Dark Night.* Pittsburgh, PA: Epiphany Books, 2000.

_____. *Late Have I Loved Thee: The Recovery of Intimacy.* New York, NY: Crossroad, 1995.

_____. *Pathways of Spiritual Living.* Pittsburgh, PA: Epiphany Books, 2004.

_____. *Praying the Lord's Prayer with Mary.* Totowa, NJ: Resurrection Press, 2001.

Muto, Susan and Adrian van Kaam. *The Commandments: Ten Ways to a Happy Life and a Healthy Soul.* Ann Arbor, MI: Servant Publications, 1996.

_____ and Adrian van Kaam. *Commitment: Key to Christian Maturity.* (Workbook and Study Guide Combined.) Pittsburgh, PA: Epiphany Books, 2002.

_____ and Adrian van Kaam. *Divine Guidance: Seeking to Find and Follow the Will of God*. Pittsburgh, PA: Epiphany Books, 2000.

_____ and Adrian van Kaam. *Harnessing Stress: A Spiritual Quest*. Pittsburgh, PA: Epiphany Books, 2003.

_____ and Adrian van Kaam. *Healthy and Holy Under Stress: A Royal Road to Wise Living*. Totowa, NJ: Resurrection Press, 1993.

_____ and Adrian van Kaam. *Practicing the Prayer of Presence*. Totowa, NJ: Resurrection Press, 1993.

_____ and Adrian van Kaam. *Stress and the Search for Happiness: A New Challenge for Christian Spirituality*. Pittsburgh, PA: Epiphany Books, 1993.

_____ and Adrian van Kaam. *The Woman's Guide to the Catechism of the Catholic Church*. Ann Arbor, MI: Servant, 1997.

Nouwen, Henri J. M. *The Wounded Healer: Ministry in Contemporary Society*. Garden City, NY: Doubleday, 1972.

John Paul II. *Crossing the Threshold of Hope*. New York, NY: Alfred A. Knopf, 1994.

Teresa of Avila. *The Book of Her Life in The Collected Works*. Vol. 1, Trans. Kieran Kavanaugh, and Otilio Rodriguez. Second Ed. Rev. Washington, DC: ICS Publications, 1987.

Teresa of Avila. *Let Nothing Trouble You*. Comp. Heidi Hess. Ann Arbor, MI: Servant Publications, 1998.

van Kaam, Adrian. *Formation of the Human Heart*. Volume 3, Formative Spirituality. New York NY: Crossroad, 1991.

_____. *The Music of Eternity*. Notre Dame, IN: Ave Maria Press, 1990.

_____. *Spirituality and the Gentle Life*. Pittsburgh, PA: Epiphany Association, 1994.

_____. *The Tender Farewell of Jesus: Meditations on Chapter 17 of John's Gospel*. Hyde Park, NY: New City Press, 1996.

_____. *Transcendence Therapy. Formative Spirituality Series.* Volume VII. New York, NY: Crossroad, 1995.

van Kaam, Adrian and Susan Muto. *Dynamics of Spiritual Direction.* Revised Edition. Pittsburgh, PA: Epiphany Books, 2003.

_____ and Susan Muto. *Formation Guide for Becoming Spiritually Mature.* Pittsburgh, PA: Epiphany Books, 1991.

_____ and Susan Muto. *The Emergent Self.* Pittsburgh, PA: Epiphany Books, 2003.

_____ and Susan Muto. *The Power of Appreciation: A New Approach to Personal and Relational Healing.* Pittsburgh, PA: Epiphany Books, 1999.

van Zeller, Dom Hubert. *Holiness for Housewives.* Manchester, NH: Sophia Institute Press, 1997.

---

Books by Adrian van Kaam and Susan Muto
can be ordered from the
Epiphany Academy of Formative Spirituality

To order please call
1-877-324-6873

---

# About the Authors

Father Adrian van Kaam, C.S.Sp., Ph.D., is the originator of formation science and its underlying formation anthropology. These new disciplines serve his systematic and systemic formation theology. Taken as a whole, all three fields comprise the art and discipline he named formative spirituality.

He inaugurated this unique approach in Holland in the 1940's. Upon coming to the United States in 1954, he went to Case Western Reserve University in Cleveland where he received his doctorate in psychology. Shortly thereafter he became an American citizen.

From 1954 to 1963, he taught his original approach to psychology as a human science at Duquesne University. Then in 1963 he founded the Graduate Institute of Formative Spirituality, received the President's Award for excellence in research, and taught there as a professor in this field until its closing in 1993. He is also the recipient of an honorary Doctor of Christian Letters degree from the Franciscan University of Steubenville, Ohio.

The author of numerous books on spiritual formation, an inspiration to many, a renowned speaker, a prolific poet, Father Adrian's work enjoys worldwide recognition.

Susan Muto, Ph.D., who received her doctorate in English Literature from the University of Pittsburgh, is executive director and co-founder of the Epiphany Association. Professor Muto, an expert in the comprehensive field of formative spirituality with a special emphasis on scripture and the Christian classics, teaches her original courses, conferences, seminars, and workshops for laity, clergy, and religious at the Epiphany Academy and at seminaries, colleges, and institutes of higher learning in the United States and abroad.

Author of many books, poems, and articles, Doctor Muto is the recipient of an honorary Doctor of Humanities degree from King's College and the President's Award for excellence in teaching at the Institute of Formative Spirituality (IFS), formerly sponsored by Duquesne University. She is a renowned speaker, an inspiring teacher, a dedicated single lay woman, whose ministry serves many people in the Church and in the world.

# OTHER BOOKS OF INTEREST

## PRAYING THE LORD'S PRAYER WITH MARY
### An Imaginative Meditation
### Susan Muto and Adrian vanKaam

"... wipes away our preconceived notions and reveals the truly revolutionary nature of the Lord's prayer." —**Catholic Library World**

**No. RP 150/04**  ISBN 1-878718-67-3                              **$8.95**

## YOU ARE MY BELOVED
### Meditations on God's Steadfast Love

"With the humor and candor of a wise friend. Mitch Finley strips away all our fears, defenses, and foolishness to point out the joy and opportunity in acknowledging and gracefully accepting God's limitless love for us."                              —**Ron Hansen**

*Comes with 4-color bookmark

**No. RP 115/04**  ISBN 1-878718-49-5                              **$10.95**

## BLESSINGS ALL AROUND US
### Savoring God's Gifts
### Dolores Leckey

"... the reader will be challenged to pray and ponder the scriptures ... to experience the beauty of leisure and the significance of family and friends. "                              —**Bishop Robert F. Morneau**

**No. RP 119/04**  ISBN 1-878718-50-9                              **$8.95**

## SOMETIMES I HAVEN'T GOT A PRAYER
### ... And Other "Real" Catholic Adventures
### Mary Kavanagh Sherry

"... down-to-earth, even extremely funny, and filled with insights born of love and lighthearted determination to be a growing yet faithful believer committed to Catholicism." —**Dominican Vision**

**No. RP 174/04**  ISBN 1-878718-79-7                              **$8.95**

## DISCERNMENT
### Seeking God in Every Situation
### Rev. Chris Aridas

"This is a book to cherish. It should be read slowly and prayerfully. Then it can be re-read again and again, providing special nourishment for those who take their spiritual journey seriously."
—**Robert E. Lauder**

**No. RP 194/04**  ISBN 1-878718-88-6                              **$8.95**

## *www.catholicbookpublishing.com*

## THE JOY OF MUSIC MINISTRY
### John Michael Talbot
"I encourage every pastor, musician, parish staff member, . . . to read this book."
—Fr. Dale Fushek

No. RP145/04   ISBN 1-878718-63-0   $6.95

## THE JOY OF BEING A LECTOR
### Mitch Finley

". . . practical, full of useful suggestions on how to be a better lector."
—Fr. Joseph Champlin
No. RP123/04   ISBN 1-878718-57-6   $5.95
Also Available in Spanish: La Alegria De Ser Lector   No. RPS 123/04   $5.95

## THE JOY OF BEING A CATECHIST
### Gloria Durka, Ph.D.

"Chock-full of suggestions both practical and spiritual for gaining or maintaining our visions . . . perfect end-of-year gift."
—Religion Teachers Journal
No. RP520/04   ISBN 1-878718-27-4   $4.95
Also Available in Spanish: La Alegria De Ser Catequista   RPS520/04   $4.95

## THE JOY OF TEACHING
### Joanmarie Smith, C.S.J.

". . . a lovely gift book for all proclaimers of the gospel."   —Religion Teachers Journal
No. RP114/04   ISBN 1-878718-44-4   $5.95
Also Available in Spanish:  La Alegria De Ser Educador—RPS114/04

## THE JOY OF PREACHING
### Fr. Rod Damico
"A gem . . . should be read by every deacon and candidate."   —Deacon Jerry Wilson
No. RP142/04   ISBN 1-878718-61-4   $6.95

## THE JOY OF BEING A EUCHARISTIC MINISTER
### Mitch Finley

". . . provides insights meant to deepen one's relationship to the risen Christ."
—St. Anthony Messenger
No. RP010/04   ISBN 1-878718-45-2   $5.95
Also Available in Spanish: La Alegria De Ser Ministro De La Eucaristia—RPS010/04

## THE JOY OF MARRIAGE PREPARATION
### Tony Marinelli and Pat McDonough
". . . will benefit not only those who prepare couples for marriage, but also those couples who approach this sacrament."   —Bishop Emeritus John R. McGann
No. RP148/04   ISBN 1-878718-64-9   $5.95

## THE JOY OF USHERS AND HOSPITALITY MINISTERS
### Sr. Gretchen Hailer, RSHM

". . . share ways to make your parish a place of Welcome and Thanksgiving."
No. RP328/04   ISBN 1-878718-60-6   $5.95

## THE JOY OF BEING AN ALTAR SERVER
### Joseph M. Champlin
". . .a down-to-earth, hands-on resource for servers of any age!"
No. RP162/04   ISBN 1-878718-66-5   $5.95

# 1-800-892-6657

# Additional Titles Published by Resurrection Press, a Catholic Book Publishing Imprint

For a free catalog call 1-800-892-6657

www.catholicbookpublishing.com